The Dark Side of Sunshine

By Paul Guzzo

Aignos Publishing, Inc.

Honolulu, Hawaii
2012

Published in the USA by Aignos Publishing, Inc.
1910 Ala Moana Blvd, #20A
Honolulu, HI 96815
www.aignospublishing.com

Printed in the USA

Extra special thank you to the wonderful people at Cigar City Magazine and La
Gaceta

Edited by Jon Marcantoni
Cover art provided by Joe Davison
Art Design by Liang-Han "Kevin" Yu

13-digit ISBN: 978-09860233-0-9
10-digit ISBN: 09860233-0-2

This book is primarily non-fictional; though information conveyed comes from
different sources, every effort has been made to assure that this work is as accurate
as possible. However, there may be mistakes, typographical and in content.
Information conveyed is current up to the date of printing.

All reprinted material is used with permission from the management of, and
represent the author's original contributions to, Cigar City Magazine and La
Gaceta.

*A*ignos Publishing, Inc.

Honolulu, Hawaii
2012

Dedication

To my Uncle Joe:

I know you would have enjoyed this book. However, even if it was written on a topic you did not like, I know that out of all my relatives outside of my immediate family, you would have been proudest of me and the first to buy it. You were always so supportive of me. You never missed a film festival in New Jersey in which my brother and I had a movie featured. You always supported our films financially in the early days when we were not yet talented enough to find investors. You were even the only one outside of my immediate family to fly to Tampa for my brother's college graduation. I hope you knew that everything you did for me and my brother was appreciated.

When you passed away suddenly and too early, I was crushed.

I tried to find a positive in your early passing and I believe this book is it. You were so kind to include me in your will. Rather than spending the money on something frivolous, I used it to help launch my freelance writing career. The first year was tough as I searched for clients, but I knew I had a financial cushion thanks to you. Today, I am proud that I earn a living solely off my writing. Without you, I would have failed in that first year and returned to a 9-5 life. If that had happened, the stories that make up this book would never have been penned. Even in death, you were my greatest supporter.

I still miss you.

Forward

It is with a profound sense of relief that I sit down to write a few lines of fulsome praise for a master work by Paul Guzzo.

I am now 84 years old and I was getting nervous about living long enough to read a master history about some of Tampa's colorful characters before I die. I also worried that I would not live long enough to read Paul Guzzo's first masterful book.

Thankfully, this book takes care of both fears.

A strong masterpiece of storytelling it features tales of men from a small section of the United States that may have been lost forever if not documented in this book. Tampa has always been equal to Dodge City, Laredo, Deadwood and all those dusty cow towns of the Old West. Finally, people can learn why I have long felt this way. Guzzo, encouraged by me yelling and hollering to do this book, has put together an exciting account of Tampa's darker side.

I received this book at suppertime and sat down and excitedly read it from 6 p.m. to 9 a.m. When I closed the book, my eyes burning, a sense of happiness that Guzzo exceeded my expectations overcame me. Everyone who should be in this book is in this book, from Charlie Wall to Bobby Rodriguez. Get ready to read a great book on Florida history.

- Dr. Ferdie Pacheco

A Note from the Author

This book is a collection of stories I have written over the years on some of Tampa's most colorful and darkest characters. Most were published in Cigar City Magazine (CCM) and one was published in La Gaceta Newspaper.

I am proud that some of these topics have never been written about before while others have never been covered in such depth. That is a testament to the two publications – CCM and La Gaceta – as using their names opened up doors not available to most writers. People were willing to tell me things they would not tell other writers simply because of the publications listed on my resume.

I hope you all enjoy this book.

-   Paul Guzzo

Chapter One
The Early Years

From the beginning, Tampa was a place for gentlemen…

The known history of the city of Tampa dates back to the 1500s when the Spanish explorers arrived and discovered the area we now know as Tampa. It is a good thing they discovered it, otherwise the Tocobaga Indians who had populated that area for many years would never have known where they were. And they would also have never known what kind of savages they were. It took Spanish gentleman to point that out.

The Spanish gentleman arrived from a nation long considered to be a world power. It was a nation in the midst of its golden era in terms of architecture, art, literature and music. It was a nation with grand cathedrals. And it was a nation with a powerful armada and king who had divine rule stating he could conquer nations beneath Spain.

The Tocobaga Indians were the type of savage race the Spaniards had a duty to conquer. These natives lived in crudely built homes made of wooden posts and covered with palm leaves. They used shells as plates and spoons. They dressed in nary an article of clothing during the hot summer months, and, worse of all, they did not believe in the Spaniards' Christian God. The horror these Spaniards, sons of Adam and Eve, must have felt when they met these half naked heathens living side by side with nature who did not believe in the Garden of Paradise.

Disgusted with these heathens and shocked that they would not be easily converted to their religion, the gentlemanly Spaniards thought of conquering them. When the Spaniards realized that, despite the natives not having God or the advanced weaponry of the Spaniards on their side, conquering them would be no easy task, they decided to leave the Tocobaga Indians to their savage ways and return to Spain. But, before they sailed home, the Spaniards left the natives with a very special present – European diseases that their bodies were not equipped to handle. These diseases wiped out the Tocobaga Indians. Their culture disappeared forever, while the gentlemanly Spaniards flourished; sailing the world, discovering land that was already inhabited and forcing their culture and religion on to savages everywhere, as only gentlemen would do.

The area now known as Tampa remained relatively unpopulated for hundreds of years until the Seminole Indians made it their home in the 1700s. In the 1800s, the gentlemanly United States purchased the land from Spain and set out to make it a proper place to live, the type of place that gentlemen would want to call home. The United States was a new nation and was still learning how to be gentleman. They fought the Revolutionary War against the British in the name of freedom of speech and religion. Soon after they won, however, they realized how silly such a notion is, how ungentlemanly it is, and learned that the only way to become true gentlemen is to look down upon and act violently toward those who are different.

In order for the United Stated to turn the area now known as Tampa into a gentlemanly community, the Americans followed the Spaniard's gentlemanly lead and decided to eradicate the savages from the land. It was, after all, their only option. Being savages, the Seminole Indians did not understand world law. They were unaware that the Spaniards owned that land because they had discovered it 300 years ago. They were unaware that the fact that their families had made it their home for over a century did not matter. They were unaware that simply by providing the Spaniards with a set fee that the United States could purchase the land.

Of course, how could they understand gentlemen's law? They were only savages. When the savages would not leave, the gentlemanly United States murdered as many of them as they could, forcing the Seminole Indians from the land in a gentlemanly fashion.

There was one other major problem in the Tampa area. It was cut off from the rest of the nation, making it difficult to establish prosperous industries. Trade is necessary for industries to grow but is impossible without a route to carry goods.

Then, in 1884, railroad tycoon Henry Plant erected a railroad line across central Florida that connected Tampa to the rest of the state. This project brought a financial windfall to the area, allowing local fisherman and phosphate miners to transport their goods throughout Florida. It also allowed tourists to visit Tampa. Seeing that there was money to be made off those seeking a getaway to Tampa's tropical climate, Henry Plant constructed one of the most lavish hotels in the nation, doing so along his railroad line and aptly naming it the Tampa Bay Hotel. This hotel set the standards for how Tampa's forefathers wanted their city built – extravagantly, the type of place a lady and gentleman would feel comfortable.

The Tampa Bay Hotel was a 500-plus room luxury resort that boasted exotic artwork from around the world and Moorish architecture that boasted six minarets, four cupolas and three domes. It also had the first electric lights in Tampa and the first elevator and phones in Florida. The total cost to build the hotel was $2.5 million, a king's ransom by that time's standards, and rooms rented for as much as $15 a night, which was a price only the highest of class could afford. The hotel grounds also included a plethora of upper class activities, such as a golf course, bowling alley, racetrack, casino and an indoor heated swimming pool. At night, the hotel's music room would open its windows, all of which doubled as doorways leading to the front patio. An orchestra would perform on stage while guests waltzed in line, dancing through the doorway windows, back and forth, between the inside and outside, until the wee hours of the morning. That was how ladies and gentlemen lived.

A new problem was on the horizon, however, one that threatened the gentlemanly existence they had created – Latin immigrants were populating an area located on the outskirts of Tampa. They were not gentlemen, a nd t heir manner of living proved it.

The area they inhabited was called Ybor City after its founder, Vicente Ybor, who in 1885 established the cigar industry in that section of town. It was a savage area, filled with w ild a nimals, p almettos a nd g uava. M ost o f t he immigrants were uneducated men and women who earned livings in the blue collar t rade of c igar rolling. Their initial roads were made of dirt and their homes were s plintered s hacks. The Caucasians worried that t hese savages would try to cohabitate Tampa, so they forbid them from entering their establishments.

However, as the city of Tampa continued to grow, the gentlemanly forefathers realized that their tax base was not large enough to support their vision of Tampa. So, in 1 887, t hey annexed Ybor City. While these immigrants were not gentlemanly enough to visit the Caucasian establishments, their money was good enough to support the city. Those forefathers with the gentlemanly idea to exploit these savages were wise.

Following the completion of Vicente Ybor's three-story cigar factory, which was t he largest in t he world at t he time, immigrants from Cuba a nd Spain who made their living in the cigar industry flocked to Ybor City for work. Other cigar factory owners s oon opened m ore factories i n the area. I mmigrants from Italy and Germany also flocked to Ybor City, opening industries that could support the community, s uch as merchant s hops. Ybor City went on to become the cigar capital of the world, earning the City of Tampa a great deal of money.

Ybor City also went on to become gentlemanly in its own right. Spurned by the Caucasian community, they decided to build a community that could sustain itself and did so mimicking t heir g entlemanly Caucasian n eighbors. The respective cultures each founded a mutual aid s ociety – Cuban Club, Italian Club, Centro Español (Spain) a nd Centro A sturiano (Asturias, S pain) – that o ffered its members a medical clinic, bank, burial services and live entertainment in the form of dances, theatre shows and concerts. And each mutual aid society was housed in buildings whose s ize was only dwarfed by their architecture, each built as grandly as the Tampa Bay Hotel. Though lower class in status, the immigrants sought to mimic their gentlemanly Caucasian neighbors in other ways. They too treated members of their community as second class citizens.

In Ybor City, those with darker features were forbidden from being members of the social clubs. The Afro-Cubans, the only heavily populated group of dark skinned immigrants living in Ybor City in its early days, were tossed out of the Cuban Club, forced to build their own mutual aid society – La Union Marti-Maceo – in 1900. Also, the cigar factory owners treated their employees as substandard human beings, providing them with minimal wages and poor working conditions. When the cigar factory workers went on strike, the gentlemanly factory owners did what any gentleman would do – they went back to their high income homes and ate lavish meals until the poor cigar workers caved on their demands due to hunger pains in their own children's bellies.

Once the Afro-Cubans were ostracized and the blue collar workers were put in their place, Ybor City officially became a place where a proper gentleman could reside.

The Caucasians and the immigrants lived side by side, each working to build communities that could be deemed as perfect, civil and, of course, gentlemanly.

There are some who believe the Holocaust never happened. They claim that the photographs of Jews with decimated bodies were doctored, the newsreels showing piles of bones belonging to exterminated Jews are fakes, the newspaper clippings with headlines about the human ovens that were used to cook the Jews were written by journalists who were trying to advance the interest of the Jews at the expense of the Germans, and the history books documenting the horrors of the concentration camps are penned by fools, men and women dumb enough to fall for such lies.

This is what is called historical "denialism". It is easier to deny that dark times occurred than to try to rationalize why people acted in such a manner.

While Tampa obviously does not deny any wrong doings that are on the same level as the Holocaust, the city is guilty of the crime of historical denialism nonetheless. For years, historians have painted Tampa as a perfect little town where everyone worked side by side for the betterment of the community, where neighbors boked out for neighbors, and where everyone bved everyone. The truth is, Tampa was like every other city in the world – it had as much darkness as it did sunshine.

Tampa's history can be divided into three dark eras – the early years of danger, where the greatest fear was the nightmarish individuals who were allowed to roam the nights in a city without a proper law enforcement organization in place; the mid-1900s when one of the most power criminal syndicates in the nation made its home in Tampa and when a another nation's revolutionary war affected the city's residents; and the late 1900s to early 2000s when Tampa became a sexual playground. Each flows effortlessly into the next, one always passing the torch to the next. These eras can be denied, but they cannot be hidden, nor should they be. By ignoring these dark times, history is either omitted or falsely told.

If those who tried to silence free speech are ignored, how can we appreciate those who fought to preserve it?

If the era of fixed elections through ballot box stuffing in Tampa is ignored, how would people understand why the invention of the lever voting machine was so important?

If the gangsters who constantly worked to outsmart law enforcement are swept under the rug, the groundbreaking technologies used to catch these criminals would be ignored.

And if the dangerous individuals in Tampa who once stalked the nights during the early years are treated as fake boogeymen, the courage it took for the founders of Tampa to establish a community in a wild and lawless land would be overlooked.

It is with one of those dangerous individuals in which our story will begin. In the shadows lie people looking to use fear to destroy all that the forefathers were trying to build. Lurking in the shadows were murderers who killed purely for the sake of killing.

The first and perhaps most dangerous of these men was Robert Anderson, otherwise known as "The Firebug."

Chapter Two
A Serial Killer in Ybor

For seven long months in 1912, Robert Anderson, aka "The Firebug", aka "The Killer", held Ybor City in a prison of fear. The men, women, and children of Ybor City were afraid to go outside. They were even afraid to close their eyes at night. They wanted to hide inside, away from windows, away from the light, away from the eyes of "The Killer," and they wanted to be on constant vigil in case he decided to enter their residence and make them or their home his next victim.

A century later, few people seem to know about this dark period in Ybor City's history; few people seem to know that their beloved historic district was once home to one of the nation's first serial killers.

The first of a string of then-unsolved homicides began in 1911 on Christmas Eve day when police found Tampa Steam Ways night watchman Leander Cutter murdered. In early 1912, police found an unidentified murdered African American man on the Seaboard tracks. On May 29, 1912, Manuel Perez was found dead near the Hendry & Knight docks, and on June 30, 1912 another Tampa Steam Ways night watchman, Edward Geary, was killed.

Police had no suspects for any of these murders, but there was no reason to believe they were connected. Also, it was 1912 and none of the victims were white, so the crimes were lost in the middle of the newspapers and there was little public outcry to find the "men" behind the murders.

Then, on April 9, 1912, Robert Anderson threw an anonymous letter over the wall at the Hillsborough County Jail. Anderson wrote that he was an African American man who was angry that some white men were having relations with African American women who lived on Fifth Avenue. In the letter, he then stated that if law enforcement did not order a stop to this practice, he would burn the city to the ground.

When law enforcement did not speak out against what Anderson thought was a crime, he began mailing more letters with the same threat, sending some to the Hillsborough County Sheriff's Office and some to the Tampa Police Department. When there was still no reaction from law enforcement, in terms of either listening to his demand or simply acknowledging his existence, Anderson carried out his threat.

For two months, Ybor City burned. Anywhere from 50–100 fires were credited to him, most of them taking place in the African American community's lowest income neighborhoods. In most cases, the fires were started with kerosene-soaked rags placed under a bed or in a corner among rubbish, where fire fighters stated a fire could do the most harm.

None of the blazes elicited any serious damage until Anderson set fire to the original Centro Asturiano and completely destroyed the structure. It would take two years before a new building was erected.

Following the Centro Asturiano's destruction, police stepped up their hunt to find the man they referred to as "The Ybor City Firebug." With no description or name of the suspect, police arrested and questioned a handful of individuals based on circumstantial evidence but released them each shortly after questioning ended.

To make himself harder to find, Anderson turned himself into a woman. He sometimes dressed in drag when he lit fires. Witnesses began telling tales of a hideously ugly woman running from the homes moments before they erupted in flames.

While his tactics had Ybor City living in fear, law enforcement still ignored his request to stop the white men from having relations with the African American women, so he began using a more menacing approach to get attention. He traded his kerosene for a gun.

On August 9, a half white/half African American woman named Ada was shot in the foot while sitting on her front porch. She never saw the shooter but said he must have fired at her from across the street while hiding behind a tree or a house. She said she had no knowledge of anyone who wanted to hurt her and there was no warning before the shot was fired. She said she heard a loud boom, felt a stinging in her foot and then noticed she had been shot. The woman suffered only a minor injury.

On August 11, another half white/half African American woman also named Ada was shot and wounded by a phantom gunman while she was sitting on her porch. Again, the suspect escaped and again the victim said that she had no knowledge of anyone wanting to harm her. Her injuries were more serious than the first Ada's, but were not life threatening.

Police thought that someone who was looking to exact revenge on a woman named Ada was "accidentally" firing at the wrong ones. But a few days after the August 11 shooting, "The Firebug" sent an anonymous letter to law enforcement stating he was behind the shootings and that he would continue to shoot anyone he wanted until white men were banned from sleeping with African American women. He also took credit for the unsolved Christmas Eve day murder and the string of early 1912 unsolved murders, but did not explain why he took their lives. Those murders were committed before his ultimatum.

Law enforcement again ignored his outlandish request and Anderson remained true to his word.

Over the next month and a half, he shot and wounded another three individuals, two black women and another woman of mixed-race.

At some point in September, Anderson sent an anonymous letter to the Tampa Police Department stating that he was going to kill an officer. Shortly thereafter, he took aim at a police officer in an African American community bordering Ybor City that was known as The Scrubs. He yelled to the officer from down the road that he was going to murder him and opened fire, unloading four shots at the officer. He missed. The officer returned fire and chased the gunman but the pursuit ended in failure. However, the officer was able to add the suspect's height, 5'6; weight, 145 – 150; and skin tone, a "ginger black", to the description.

A few more men were arrested based on this description and released. Anderson was never amongst them. He had police completely baffled.

On September 26, at 10:30 p.m., Anderson walked into the Fourth Avenue and 15th Street home of Cuban woman Maria Louisa Rodriguez and, without warning, shot her. The bullet pierced her right side and broke a rung on the back of her chair. She died instantly. Her young son watched from the chair beside her but the shooter entered and then exited the house so briskly that he never got a clear look at him. Rodriguez' son gave chase, trying desperately to catch the man who just murdered his mother, but another pursuit ended in failure. The only description he could give was that the murderer was African American.

The following day, "The Firebug" was renamed "The Killer."

On October 3, Anderson struck again. From the street, he shot through a disorderly house's window on the corner of Governor and Kay Streets, killing one of the inmates, Viola Danford, hitting her twice in the back.

The next day, October 4, he slew Stephen Canal in front of his tiny shop on the corner of Nebraska and Fifth Avenues. He casually strolled up to the shop, took aim, fired and murdered the shopkeeper. He then just as casually strolled away and disappeared into the Tampa night before the police arrived.

Ybor City was rippling with terror. This unknown murderer was killing at will and without fear of being caught, and it seemed no one could stop him. As people walked down the street, even if in a crowd, they flinched when a loud noise echoed throughout the night, wondering if it was a gunshot meant for them.

"The Killer" needed to be brought to justice, residents cried.

Then, on October 5, police spotted a man fitting the description of "The Killer" leaning against a wall outside an Ybor City bar as though he did not have a care in the world. When he spotted the police watching him, he did not seem worried in the least. He was not acting like a guilty man. The police stood on the corner and watched him for a few moments. He then casually strolled down the street in the direction of the police. When he passed them, they grabbed him by the wrist and arrested him.

They took him to a local fire station for questioning, but he answered everything correctly and it seemed as though he was not the killer. One detective, however, had a feeling that something was amiss and asked if they could search his home. For some reason, he agreed.

He led officers to a room he rented in a tenant home in The Scrubs and, as the officers rummaged through his things, looking for evidence, they took their eyes off Anderson for just an instant, which was enough time for him to make his move. He dashed out the door and disappeared into the city. The police chased him but could not find him. "The Killer" had escaped.

When the police later returned to his rental room, they realized why he ran. They found a gun matching the bullets used at one of the murders and woman's accessories, probably those he dressed in to commit the crimes.

Robert Anderson found an African American gentleman outside Tampa Gas Company who was willing to file his handcuffs off of him. He then hitchhiked to Plant City, where he hid for a short time before travelling to Mayberry, Lakeland, Sanford and finally Jacksonville.

Every law enforcement agency in the state was on the lookout for him and various rewards offered from law enforcement and private citizens totaling $2,200 were offered to whomever led police to him. In early November, he was finally captured in Jacksonville and a few days later he was brought to Tampa. On the journey back to Tampa, police were able to get Anderson to admit he was "The Killer." By the time he was caught, between 50 and 100 buildings were burned. Seven people were murdered. Several more were wounded.

His trial was quick. Though witnesses were never able to give a vivid description of him following his crimes, when they laid eyes on him in court they were able to positively state that Anderson was "The Killer." Then, when Anderson took the stand, he admitted he was "The Killer" but tried to plead insanity. It did not work. The verdict was guilty and the punishment was death by hanging.

Whether or not he truly killed and set fires because police ignored his ultimatum or because he was a maniac who just wanted to hurt others was never established. All law enforcement seemed to care about was that Anderson was off the streets.

On November 22, 1912, dressed in a black suit, white shirt with a standing collar and a black tie, he stepped upon the trap inside the confines of the Hillsborough County Jail yard without a tremor. He murmured a short prayer while the deputies adjusted the rope around his neck and placed the black cap over his head. At 11:27 a.m., Sheriff R.A. Jackson, with his hand on the trigger, said, "Robert Anderson, may God have mercy on your soul" and the confessed murderer dropped through the trap. His neck broke immediately but his body swung for eight agonizing minutes before his heart stopped. When he was cut down, onlookers divvied up the rope for souvenirs.

As the last breath was pushed out of Robert Anderson's body, all of Ybor City breathed their first sigh of relief since the nightmare began seven months earlier. Robert Anderson, aka "The Firebug," aka "The Killer" was finally gone. However, this was not the last time that terror would visit Tampa. Decades later, one Ybor City home turned into a scene that rivals any modern day horror movie.

Chapter Three
Horror in Ybor City
The Victor Licata Murders

Originally published in Cigar City Magazine Issue 27 in 2010

October 17, 1933

Blood soaked the beds and dripped off the sides, forming thick red puddles on the wooden floors of the Ybor City *casita*. Mangled and mutilated bodies were strewn throughout the house. A dying boy lay in his bed, struggling for his next breath. And under the front porch, a dog caked in its own blood let out one final whimper before joining his owners in the afterlife. Just hours before, sadistic acts turned this once peaceful home into hell on earth. Yet, no one in Ybor City knew anything was wrong.

Ybor City went about its business as usual that morning. The streetcars rumbled down their tracks laid upon the brick streets of the Latin District, dropping off the cigar workers at the factories. The cafés were filled with Latinos sipping their café con leche and arguing politics. Kids rushed off to school; the boys exclaiming that they would rule the schoolyard baseball games that day while the girls whispered about which boys they thought were cute. The clickity-clack of dominoes slamming onto tables echoed throughout the Cuban Club and Centro Asturiano. And the Seventh Avenue merchants unlocked their doors for another day of business. Everything seemed normal in Ybor City- well, almost everything.

The *casita* located at 1707 Fifth Avenue, the Licata family's home, was quiet, which was far from normal. The patriarch of the family, Michael Licata, owned two successful downtown barbershops. In the late morning hours, neighbors began to think, surely Michael should have left for work already, yet they never saw him leave the home that morning. The Licata's had two school-age children, yet the neighbors never saw them leave for school. And the family had a dog, but no one had walked it. If the Licatas had gone on vacation, they would have told somebody, whispered the neighbors. As minutes turned to an hour and there was still no noise coming from the home, neighbors finally contacted the police.

When the police arrived, they had to enter the home through a rear window; all outside doors were locked. Once inside, they found the horror that was hiding behind those locked doors.

On the bed in the front room they found Michael Licata lying in a welter of blood, killed with one swing of an axe. In the adjoining bedroom they found the bodies of the family's 22-year-old soon-to-be-married daughter, Providence, and her 8-year-old brother, Jose, both hacked to death. In the rear bedroom they found the murdered mother, 44-year-old Rosalie. On the bed beside her lay her 14-year-old son, Philip, alive but suffering from numerous axe wounds. And lying on the floor next to the bed was the murder weapon—a blood-stained axe.

After removing the dying boy from the room and getting him to the hospital, the police continued their search, finding the Licata's 21-year-old son, Victor, cowering in the bathroom, dressed in a clean white shirt and well-pressed trousers. Underneath his clean clothes, though, his naked skin was stained in blood.

Victor Licata was a tiny man—just 5'8 and 127 pounds. He was soft spoken and often described as possessing "queer manners" by friends and family. But he was long known to be dangerous and mentally unstable, so much so that his father slept with a pistol between his mattresses. A drunk and a habitual marijuana smoker, the police tried to commit Victor a year ago but his family refused, claiming t hey co uld t ake b etter ca re o f h im t hemselves. B ut t he f amily underestimated the demons that lived inside Victor. It wasn't u ntil t he police interrogated Victor that anyone truly understood how insane he'd become.

According to Victor, he didn't kill his family. Actually, he told police, his family had attacked HIM.

He told police t hat on the n ight o f October 16, 1933, h e d rove a round town on the back of a friend's truck drinking moonshine and smoking marijuana. He returned home sometime between 8 and 10 p.m. His sister was out. His mother was in the kitchen. His brothers were in bed. He said he then went to bed and fell asleep, b ut woke up a few hours later w hen h is f ather came charging into the room, pulled him from bed and held him against the wall. According to Victor, his mother then entered the room wielding a kitchen knife and jeered and taunted him as h is b rothers a nd s isters p ointed a nd laughed at h im. He said his mother then sawed o ff h is a rms with t he knife a nd jabbed h omemade wooden a rms with iron claws as h ands into h is s tumps. Victor said that when the attack ended and his family left the room, he sought revenge. He said he found an axe on the porch, but it wasn't a normal axe. He said it was a "funny axe," rubbery, like something out of a s lapstick cartoon. He s aid he then took the funny axe and whacked his family members i n their heads with it, knocking them unconscious, but never killed them. He did say, though, that when he finished the attack he found it odd when he was able to wring blood out of the axe, which "caused great pain" in his stomach.

What made this s tory even creepier was t hat Victor s eemed t o b e 1 00 percent honest when he told it. He thought it was true. Investigators believed that he had a nightmare that his family attacked him as explained. Investigators stated that they b elieved h e t hen woke u p a nd, in a delirious state, murdered his family and family dog with the axe, thus earning himself the nickname "The Dream Slayer".

Philip died i n the h ospital s oon after he was admitted and Victor was charged with the murder o f h is five family members. But, just d ays later, friends and family came to his rescue. They refused to allow him to be tried for murder, bringing insanity proceedings against him in Civil Court.

Family and friends claimed that Victor's insanity was due to his habitual marijuana use. But, according to a court-appointed commission's report, the axe-murderer suffered from a form of dementia. In fact, his brother Philip was also pronounced to be a victim of dementia. Victor also had a grand-uncle who died in an asylum and two cousins who were in asylums at the time of the murder. Finally, the commission discovered that Victor's parents—Michael and Rosalie—were first cousins.

Following the release of the report, the state attorney announced he would not even indict Victor with murder, saying that it would be a waste of money to try someone with murder who was "definitely established" as insane. Victor was instead given a life sentence at a mental institution in Chattahoochee, Florida with no parole. Victor, though, didn't need parole. He found another way out of the institution.

On October 15, 1945–just one day short of the 12-year-anniversary of the Licata murders—Victor's cell at the institution was found empty. Victor, along with four other patients, had escaped.

One of the escaped inmates was caught just hours after the empty cells were found and claimed that they sawed the iron bars from a cell window with a piece of tin and climbed to freedom. One of the institution's attendants swore he checked the bars hours before the escape and they were fully intact. But, investigators said it was impossible for a piece of tin to cut through iron bars and that even with a hacksaw it would have taken days to do so, not mere hours. Investigators said the escape was made possible through inside help.

According to investigators, the escapees obtained cellblock keys from one of the attendants and used them to meet in the same cellblock. For how many nights they met is unknown, but they met enough times to saw the bars from a window in that cellblock; though never completely sawing them away, as doing so would have been noticeable. Instead, they sawed them to the point that they could remain intact but be easily broken when they were ready to escape. On the night they escaped, they broke the sawed bars away from the window and climbed down a ladder made of sheets.

Four of the five fugitives were quickly found; Licata successfully escaped the c ounty. A n a xe-murderer was on the loose. And, to compound matters, cellmates s tated t hat Victor h ad recently b een t alking a bout his des ire to murder every member of his family.

Five years later he may have tried to make good on that desire.

In A ugust 1 950, V ictor c asually w alked i nto h is Cousin Philip's restaurant in New Orleans, telling his cousin that he had been working as a laborer in L ouisiana for t he past nine months and as a laborer in Texas and Delaware before that. Philip p layed it c ool, fixing Victor d inner a nd then buying him a few beers at a bar across the street. He then told Victor that he needed to go home, but asked him to come back the next day.

"I was afraid of him, all right, the way y ou'd be afraid of any crazy man," Philip later t old t he media. "I d ecided I'd g et h im to come back the next day and I'd have police waiting for him."

Victor d id return the n ext day and spent three hours talking to the short order cook, but he disappeared before the police arrived.

He returned to the restaurant for a third time the following day, and this time his cousin wasn't going to let him get away. Philip waited for Victor to turn his b ack a nd then p ounced o n h im, p inning h is t iny cousin to the wall until the police arrived.

Upon his arrest, Victor was ordered to the Florida State Prison in Raiford until a court could decide where he should permanently reside. But, again, Victor had other plans.

In December 1950, a prison guard f ound V ictor's s till w arm b ody dangling from a bed sheet tied to the top of his cell's double-decked bed. According to investigators, shortly after his cellmate went to the yard for exercise, Victor committed suicide by hanging, the final c hapter in the b loody Ybor City story o f the "Dream S layer," OR, so everyone thought. Actually, the ghost of Michael Licata haunts the entire nation to this day

In an e ffort t o justify the c riminalization o f marijuana, H enry A nslinger, who President H oover n amed h ead o f t he n ewly-formed F ederal B ureau o f Narcotics in 1930, set out to prove that marijuana caused normally rational people to turn into violent c riminals. A nslinger s tarted a mass media c ampaign, writing articles documenting cases of marijuana-induced violence for n ewspapers a nd magazines across the country, a series of articles that has become famously known as the "Gore File."

The file included a total of 200 stories, ranging from a young woman who claimed s he murdered a bus driver in cold blood while high on marijuana; a child rapist who said marijuana made him do it; and a young man who said he murdered his entire family with an axe b ecause h e was h igh on marijuana. This p articular axe-murderer was Ybor City resident Victor Licata and his tale of slaughtering his parents, s ister and two b rothers was the b ackbone of Anslinger's anti-marijuana crusade.

"An entire family was murdered by a y outhful addict in Florida," wrote Anslinger. "When officers arrived at the home, they found the youth staggering about in a human slaughterhouse. With an axe he had killed his father, mother, two brothers and a sister. He seemed to be in a daze...He had no recollection of having committed the multiple crimes. The officers knew h im ordinarily as a sane, rather quiet young man; now he was pitifully crazed. They sought the reason. The boy said that he had been in the habit of smoking something which youthful friends called 'muggles,' a childish name for marijuana."

Anslinger t estified before Congress in 1937 that marijuana caused Victor Licata to murder his family and that if marijuana was not criminalized, more families could suffer the same fate. With a p ublic s well of s upport b ehind h im, Anslinger convinced C ongress t o p ass t he first federal a nti-marijuana a ct–The Marijuana Tax Act of 1937. The act levied a token tax of approximately one dollar on all buyers, sellers, importers, growers, physicians, veterinarians, and any other persons who dealt in marijuana commercially, prescribed it professionally, or possessed it. The purpose? To tax medical practices and companies that used hemp for clothing out of business. But, it had larger ramifications– it set a precedent that marijuana was a d anger to s ociety, leading to future laws that made all marijuana use illegal.

There is j ust o ne p roblem w ith A nslinger's s tory–marijuana h ad NOTHING to do with the murders. Licata d id admit to the police that he smoked marijuana the night of the murders. But the report also stated that Licata was long thought to be mentally unstable. He suffered from dementia, his family had a history of mental instability, and his parents were first cousins. Nowhere in the report was marijuana mentioned as a cause of Licata's mental instability.

Recently, researchers were able to prove that 198 of the 200 marijuana-induced violent crimes documented in the "Gore File" were erroneously blamed on marijuana use. Researchers couldn't prove the remaining two false stories because no records of the crimes even existed.

It is of no matter today, as Anslinger was successful. Today, marijuana remains criminal and Victor Licata's horrific and pointless crime is a major reason for it.

In the years directly following the Licata bloodbath, seemingly enough blood was spilled in Tampa to fill the Hillsborough River. Many of these murders were not pointless, however. There was a reason behind them – POWER.

Chapter 4
The Devil Looks After His Own

Charlie Wall

Above, a rare photo taken of Charlie Wall as a young man.

Originally published in Cigar City Magazine Issue 35 in 2011

April 19, 1955

Almost every squad car in Hillsborough County, Florida was lined up around the block. A crowd of men, women and children stood anxiously in the yard of the only mansion in the Tampa community of Ybor City, waiting to hear if the news was true. Rumors of another gang slaying had spread throughout the city. While gang slayings had become a norm in Tampa, this latest being the 21st in the last 23 years, this slaying was different. This murder was especially brutal. The victim's neck was slashed. His head was crushed with both a blackjack and a baseball bat. Most importantly, though, was the identity of the victim. He was not just any Mafioso or gang member, the victim was one of the most colorful and notorious men in the history of Tampa, the man known as the White Shadow – Charlie Wall – the tall Anglo retired crime lord who ruled Tampa through both love and fear for most of the early part of the 20th century.

Charlie Wall used to say that he survived as long as he did because the "devil looks after his own." And, for over three decades, the devil kept a close watch on Charlie Wall, during which time he controlled the city of Tampa in a way that no individual had done before or has done since. But on April 19, 1955, the devil must have found someone else to look after, and the life of one of Tampa's most colorful figures came to a dark end.

Charlie Wall–the name elicits powerfully excited responses from those in Tampa who remember him from their childhood years in Tampa or whose parents and grandparents told them stories of him. He was the White Shadow, Tampa's original crime lord, Tampa's answer to Al Capone, John Gotti, and Lucky Luciano. He was Tampa's original Godfather. It seems everyone who was alive during Charlie Wall's reign as Tampa's underworld kingpin has a romantic story to tell about the gangster–how he thumbed his nose at the life of luxury he was born into to go into business with the dregs of society; how he gave candy and money to the neighborhood children; how he survived multiple assassination attempts; how he'd stroll down Seventh Avenue in his pristine white suit, flipping a coin in the air; how he'd lean on his cane and tip his hat to every beautiful woman he passed; and, of course, how he ran Tampa's illegal lottery, bolita.

But, outside of these general tidbits, few know the whole story of Charlie Wall and the detailed facts behind his life and reign over Tampa, which is a shame, considering that few individuals had a larger influence over Tampa's history than Charlie Wall. He fixed countless elections in Tampa for over three decades. He financially backed the cigar workers during the famous strikes. He turned Tampa into the Southern version of the Wild West, with whorehouses and gambling parlors on seemingly every corner in Ybor City and West Tampa and shootouts in broad daylight. He owned politicians, law enforcement officials, and judges. The romantic stories people remember about Charlie Wall always revolve around how he controlled Tampa's underworld, which highly underestimates his life. He owned more than the underworld. For over three decades, Charlie Wall owned Tampa.

Charlie Wall's roots can be traced back as early as the mid-1840s to his grandfather, Perry Wall, a pioneer who migrated south during the second Seminole War. Perry Wall settled in the highlands of Hernando County just north of Brooksville and went on to establish a successful career, first as a probate judge and later as postmaster.

Perry Wall's children all grew into successful adults, but none more successful than John P. Wall. John P. Wall became a doctor and served for the Confederacy during the Civil War. He was not in favor of the Confederacy's cause, but felt he couldn't turn his back on wounded soldiers simply because of their political beliefs. When the war was over, he turned to research and in 1873 became the first American doctor to conclude that yellow fever was carried by mosquitoes. He later founded the first hospital focusing solely on serving yellow fever patients.

John P. Wall was also a successful writer and politician. He was associate editor of the *Sunland Tribune*, which later became the *Tampa Tribune*; served as mayor of Tampa from 1878–1880; mapped out many of the routes through the Florida wilderness that are used by the Florida highway system today; and assisted Vicente Martinez Ybor in establishing Ybor City.

With such credentials, it's easy to see why John P. Wall was able to win the heart of Matilda McKay, a member of the famous McKay family, one of the richest families in the state of Florida and a founding family of Tampa. John P. Wall and Matilda McKay were married in 1872. Shortly thereafter, Matilda McKay's sister married into the Lykes family, another of Tampa's founding families, uniting three of Tampa's most powerful families–the Walls, McKays, and Lykes.

John and Matilda gave birth to one son—Charlie, in March 1880. With his family's money and credentials behind him, Charlie Wall had the world at his feet. Unfortunately, his would-be perfect life took a turn for the worse early on.

Matilda passed away in 1893. Just six months later, John P. Wall married his housekeeper, Louise Williams. John P. Wall's career as a doctor and politician often took him away from home for extended periods of time, leaving young Charlie with his new stepmom, a woman he grew to hate for her lavish spending of his father's money. Then, in April 1895, John P. Wall passed away. Louise Williams was now Charlie's official guardian. Upon inheriting a portion of the Wall fortune, her lifestyle became even more extravagant—she'd wear ostrich-feathered hats and would bedeck herself in jewels. The more she spent the more obstinate young Charlie became towards her. It is not sexy, but it seems to be true – Tampa's original godfather chose the life of crime because he came from a broken home.

In order to avoid her altogether, young Charlie began staying away from home for days and weeks at a time, sleeping in ditches by night and hanging out in saloons, gambling houses and whorehouses—the only places that would allow a young runaway to stick around without lecturing him. Some of the criminals who were regulars at these establishments of ill-repute grew fond of the scrappy young kid who hung around the adults. They began teaching him their trades, and, with that, Charlie Wall's life in crime began.

At the age of 12, tired of his stepmother, he shot her with a .22 rifle and wounded her. His uncle sent him to Bingham Military School in North Carolina. A romanticized story about young Charlie claims he was expelled for hanging around gambling and whorehouses in North Carolina. While he was expelled during his first year at the military school, according to school records, it was for the unromantic crime of cheating on a test.

Upon expulsion, he returned to Tampa and, with no consistent parental supervision, also returned to the seedy establishments that took him in prior to his stint in military school. By the age of 14 or 15, young Charlie was dealing craps in a casino in Fort Brooke and running numbers for some of the larger bolita dealers in Tampa who saw great potential in a criminally minded boy with white collar ties. With the last name of Wall, Charlie could get into places common criminals could not– country clubs, five-star restaurants, upscale bars and even City Hall– and sell bolita numbers.

Bolita was the illegal lottery of Tampa, a prelude to today's legal lottery. One hundred little wooden or ivory balls numbered 1 thru 100 would be placed in a bag and gamblers would bet on what number or three numbers would be pulled. Though he lacked a formal education, Charlie Wall was an intelligent businessman, even as a teenager. He saved every penny he could and as his bankroll grew, he ceased working as a runner for bolita dealers and began bankrolling bootleg liquor operations and his own bolita games. With a payoff of 85-1, a winning number would pay big dividends to the winner.

Everyone in Tampa was playing–the rich and poor; black, white and Latin; men and women. In 1927, over 300 bolita parlors were located in Tampa and an estimated 1,200 bolita parlors infiltrated every segment of Tampa. In 1927, over $20 million was played on the game. Bolita was able to flourish in such a way because the police and politicians allowed it–and the reason they allowed it was because of Charlie Wall.

Wall's major play came in 1910 when the cigar workers went on strike. Supportive of their cause, Charlie Wall financially backed the struggling cigar workers. He bought them food and paid for their medical bills so they could continue the strike. Though in the end they lost, the cigar workers forever after had an undying love for Wall. It was because of that good deed he was nicknamed "La Sombra Blanca," or "The White Shadow," meaning "The Protector."

Knowing he had the full support of the blue collar men and women of Ybor City and West Tampa, Wall made his move. He began backing political candidates, promising them he could deliver the votes of West Tampa and Ybor City. His many supporters would vote for whomever he told them to, and would look the other way when Wall had the ballot boxes stuffed or had individuals vote for his candidates up to 10 times. In return for his support, candidates had to allow Wall's bolita parlors and brothels to operate, unbothered. And, if there was an illegal operation in Tampa not backed by Wall, he'd have the police shut it down, forcing almost every gambling parlor and whorehouse in the city to give Wall a portion of their business. Some bolita parlors brought in $57,000 on a good night with Wall taking h ome h alf o f it. To add to his riches, Wall would h ave b olita games fixed to ensure a highly wagered-upon number wouldn't win. Bolita dealers would fill balls with lead so they would sink to the bottom or freeze a ball so it would be easy to find in the bag.

Of course, with great power comes great risk. He refused to live his life in fear, though. Rather than building a home in the countryside, away from the danger, he built a mansion in Ybor City, which made him an easy target. Hitmen hired by opposing gangsters would drive by his house and take shots at him as he sat on his porch or pulled into his driveway. He wasn't an idiot, though. He didn't

just build a mansion. He built a fortress. H is p orch, w here h e liked to sit and read the paper on a nice day, had two giant pillars built i nto i t, l arge e nough f or him to s afely duck behind when shots were fired. And h is garage had a metal tunnel leading from it to his house. I f hitmen were following h im h ome, a ll he needed to do was escape into his garage and he could safely make it i nto h is h ome, w here t hird-floor w indows w ere a dorned with g un r acks s o h e could return fire.

Assassination attempts became a r egular p art o f t he workday for Wall. T ales o f his exciting escapes from sure death are legendary in Ybor City. He once dove behind a car as a hitman unloaded clips of ammunition at him, and escaped any serious

injury. On another occasion he ducked under his steering wheel as bullets ripped through his car seat, whizzing just inches over his head. His most famous escape was when his car was pinned between two hitmen on Nebraska Avenue, one in front of the car and one on the side. In order to escape, his driver and bodyguard, Baby Joe, stood on the car's running board and returned fire while driving backwards through traffic. They escaped unharmed.

But there was one enemy Wall's bodyguards couldn't protect him from—himself. Addicted to morphine, Wall's arms were covered with puncture scars. One of his drivers, "Scarface" Johnny Rivera, used to tell tales of neighbors calling him late at night, informing him that Wall was stumbling around the neighborhood in nothing but his night shirt. Rivera would always hurry over and bring his boss home.

In 1928, one of Wall's former companions, Isabella Knowles, went to him in search of morphine, complaining of withdrawal pains. Wall wrote a note for her to bring to one of his lieutenants, George "Saturday" Zarate, asking Zarate to give her what she wanted. Unknown to both of them, Knowles was working as a federal informant. Both Zarate and Wall were arrested and charged with selling narcotics.

At the trial, Wall took the stand in his own defense. He never denied he wrote the note, but said he only did so to help Isabella Knowles because she said she was suffering from withdrawal. Zarate received 10 years in prison but Wall was acquitted. In later years, he buried his morphine supply near his home and drove to Indiana for drug rehabilitation.

But, he had one addiction he could never kick—his addiction to power, an addiction that blinded him to a stark reality—there is only so far you can push the limits of corruption before someone is forced to push back.

His downfall began in 1934. Claude Pepper and Park Trammel were competing in an election for state Senate and Wall was backing Trammel. Whether Trammel asked for this support is unknown. What is known is that Charlie Wall's support guaranteed Trammel would win Ybor City and West Tampa. The only question was how many votes would Wall allow Pepper to receive? In one particular district in West Tampa, Wall decried that Pepper would only receive two votes. When all the votes were tallied statewide, Pepper lost the election by 3,000 votes. In Ybor City and West Tampa, he lost by 6,000 votes. It was Wall's high water mark–he'd won a statewide election for a candidate.

The state of Florida was embarrassed by this incident and vowed to not allow another corrupt election to occur in Tampa. The following year, 1935, D.B. McKay and Robert E. Chauncey were embroiled in a heated election for mayor of Tampa. In order to squash any corruption, the National Guard was called in to guard the ballot boxes. Even when faced with the military weapons, Wall's supporters tried to stuff the ballot boxes and total bedlam erupted throughout the city. Men and women were beaten to death in riots, poll workers were threatened, and dozens of men were arrested for repeat voting, including Wall's old friend, George "Saturday" Zarate. During the election madness, a hurricane rumbled through Florida with winds exceeding 100 miles per hour. By the time the election turmoil and the hurricane winds finally died down, the city of Tampa was in ruins in terms of infrastructure and reputation.

The election made national headlines. Embarrassed, the city finally decided it had to end the corruption. To do so, it replaced the paper ballot system with lever machines. Unable to stuff the ballot boxes, Wall could no longer handpick city leaders. No longer protected by the city and no longer untouchable, other criminal syndicates were allowed to flourish, specifically the Sicilian mafia.

In 1938, Wall's good friend and business partner Tito Rubio was gunned down in front of their gambling parlor, the Lincoln Club. Wall knew the police would have to visit the club as part of their investigation. His friends and supporters begged him to clean out all the gambling equipment and shut the club down. He refused, stating he hoped that by keeping it operational the murderer would return to come after him. The murderer never returned to the club. When the police arrived to investigate the scene of the murder and found the Lincoln Club still operating, they arrested Wall and charged him with running an illegal-gambling establishment.

Wall was again acquitted, but not before he promised to tell a grand jury everything they wanted to know about Tampa's underworld. He claimed that by doing so, he hoped it would help the police find his friend's murderer. The murderer was never found and when word got out that Wall had sung to the grand jury, his support dwindled even more. By 1940, Wall's power was usurped by the Sicilians. Around 1942 a powerless Wall left Tampa for Miami and faded into retirement. For a man accustomed to living in the public eye and being treated like a king wherever he went, his new life of obscurity was a tough pill to swallow.

Then, in 1950, the Special Committee to Investigate Organized Crime - better known as the Kefauver Committee - steamrolled through the nation. In an effort to end the organized crime racket that was taking over every major city in the United States, Senator Estes Kefauver formed a committee that travelled the nation, stopped in the nation's most corrupt cities, subpoenaed that city's most notorious individuals, and questioned them under oath about the criminal syndicate in the city. Most of the individuals called to the stand denied their roles in any corrupt activities. But, when the committee came to Tampa, one individual gladly testified about his role in the Tampa underworld–Charlie Wall.

Returning to the public eye for the first time since leaving Tampa, the retired and powerless Wall took the stand and openly discussed his former life as a crime lord in Tampa during the earlier part of the century. His quick wit, engaging personality and intriguing stories about fixing bolita games and escaping assassination attempts kept the city of Tampa hanging on his every word throughout his testimony. The next day, Wall was the talk of the town and back in the limelight. He moved back to Tampa fulltime and, though he had little power, discovered he could again be the center of attention simply by telling his old stories. While the residents of Tampa loved his stories, Tampa's Sicilian mafia grew angry because when Wall began drinking, he'd cease telling old stories and turn his attention to running down the way the Sicilians operated their illegal activities.

This went on for four years. Wall's friends continued to tell him to keep quiet or he'd soon be dead. He never listened and on April 19, 1955, he was found murdered in the bedroom of his home. His head was bashed in with a black jack and a bat and his neck was sliced from ear to ear. On the dresser in his bedroom where he was found dead was Estes Kefauver's book, Crime in America, which was a summary of his findings during the crime hearings throughout the nation.

While the police had a few suspects, including Wall's former drivers—Baby Joe and Scarface Johnny—no one was ever charged. It is believed, though, that the murderer was someone who Wall knew. There was no forced entry into the home, so Wall had to have let the killer in. There was also no sign of struggle in the house, meaning Wall trusted the killer enough to allow him into his bedroom. Wall's descendants claim the murder is not unsolved. They claim police have told them it was Joe Bedami, an Italian hit man known throughout Tampa as a man you did not want to cross. However, Bedami was never even questioned by police. Years after the Charlie Wall murder, in 1968, Bedami went out for a pack of cigarettes and was never heard from again.

It's been nearly five decades since the murder and it remains a mystery, but the legend of Charlie Wall has endured.

Traces of Charlie Wall's legacy can still be found in every corner of Tampa—in the halls of the city's municipal buildings through the names and photos of the countless city leaders he secretly helped to elect; in Ybor City's social clubs through the games of bolita still thrown for special events; or in bookstores throughout the city in novels he inspired. Throughout the city of Tampa, if you look closely at those places where the sunlight doesn't shine so bright, you'll still see traces of Charlie Wall's shadow—the White Shadow.

While Charlie Wall was by far the most powerful gangster in Tampa in the 1920s and 30s, there were other gangsters in Tampa at the time always jockeying for power, always aiming to become number one. Afraid to get mixed up in the war, though many of the murders were committed out in the open, no one would ever admit to seeing a thing.

Chapter 5
Who Murdered Florentino Martinez?

Date: August 14, 1928
Time: Shortly after 9 p.m.
Place: Outside El Dorado Café, Eighth Avenue and 14th Street in Ybor City

...surely someone had to have seen something...

Two men shouted violently at one another in a popular Ybor City café bustling with business. One of the men stormed from the room. The other soon followed. A gunshot echoed throughout the establishment. Moments later, a man lay on the sidewalk in front of the café bleeding to death from a gunshot to the abdomen.

Dozens of the café's patrons filed from the establishment, surrounding and gawking at the dying man, yet they swore that they had not seen a thing. Some even swore that they had not heard a gunshot and that the wounded man had not stepped foot inside the café that night.

It all sounded impossible. Surely, someone knew what happened.

Perhaps the old drunk man who was being held up by the bar saw something? Perhaps between sips he noticed the soon-to-be-victim enter the café and sidle up to one of its illegal gambling table games.

Perhaps the young male cigar roller knew what happened? Perhaps after he slid his wedding ring from his tobacco stained finger and smiled at the pretty lady across the room, he witnessed the argument that took place between the soon-to-be-victim and another man.

Perhaps the police officer who was in the café moments before the gunshot was fired saw something? Perhaps after he helped the booze smugglers carry that night's supply into the café and collected his payoff, he got a good look at the face of the man whom the soon-to-be-victim pursued out of the room.

Or perhaps one of the soon-to-be-victim's numerous acquaintances were privy to that night's horrific event. Maybe the brunette wearing the risqué above-the-knee-skirt who was once a regular at the victim's former café saw what happened. Maybe the devil crab vendor with yellow teeth and sun cracked eyes who had been selling him lunch for half a decade had some information. Maybe the street car conductor puffing on the cigar who'd chauffeured him around town since he was a boy could fill someone in on that evening's events. Maybe one of them saw whose finger pressed on the trigger of the gun.

Despite all the potential witnesses, no one would step up and say what happened. Everyone swore that they had not seen a thing. And there was nothing shocking about the lack of witnesses. This was how Ybor City operated back then.

America was in the midst of Prohibition, yet countless establishments in Tampa did not seem to care. A café would serve coffee and food by day, and alcohol, games of chance, women, and drugs by night. Many police were on the take. They allowed the illegal establishments to operate as long as they received their weekly payments. But, no amount of money could justify an officer ignoring a murder. It would be bad PR if word got out that an officer did not investigate a shooting. It would tip off gentlemanly officials to whom the officer truly pledged his allegiance.

If someone was shot inside a "café", the police would have had to enter it and investigate–and when they saw the booze, illegal gambling, and more, they would have had to shut the place down. If the patrons wanted their favorite establishments to remain open, it was in their best interests to keep their mouths shut. The Ybor City café where the man was shot on August 14, 1928 was not just any speakeasy; it was the most popular in town–El Dorado, which was known for the best liquor, the best music, the best table games, the best dope, and the best women. No one wanted to be blamed for El Dorado being shut down.

More importantly, h owever, was t hat t his w as a lso the time period i n Ybor City when numerous gang factions violently fought over control of the city's underworld. It was almost as common to hear a gunshot at night as it was to hear dominoes clickity-clacking in the cafés in the morning. No matter how many people were wounded or murdered, few people were ever convicted of a crime. To testify against a shooter meant testifying against a member of a blood-thirsty gang. Even if someone saw their b est friend murdered, it was i n t heir b est interest t o keep their mouth shut unless they wanted to join their friend in the after-life.

When s omeone was s hot, there was a certain protocol that was followed. First, the b ody was immediately dragged out of the establishment and left in the street. Everyone inside the establishment was then told in no uncertain terms that they had not seen or heard a thing. Police were not called for one hour, giving the establishment t ime t o c lear a ll the illegal activities in case the police had to enter. With no evidence or witnesses, the crime could not be solved. The establishment remained open and no innocent bystanders had to be dealt with down the line for ratting to the police. Ybor City was a well-oiled machine when it came to covering up gang crimes.

However, on August 14, 1928, a monkey wrench was t hrown into the machine.

The v ictim, the devilishly handsome and always well-dressed 35-year-old Florentino Martinez, s omehow made his way t o his feet a nd, while h olding h is hand over his wound to stop the b leeding, was a ble to muster the s trength to stumble half a block to a medical facility, El Bien Publico Clinic. Doctors c ould not save Martinez' life. The wound was too severe for medicine in 1928. BUT, h e did live long enough to give a statement to a law enforcement officer who was not owned by one of the Ybor City gangs. According to Martinez, he was shot by a former deputy of the Hillsborough County Sheriff's Office—Roy Velasco.

It made s ense. One of the best known rivalries in all of Ybor City was the one between Velasco and Martinez and it apparently finally came to a bloody end.

The rift between the two men b egan o ver o ne y ear b efore the murder, when Velasco was straddling both sides of law enforcement fence. By day he was a deputy. By night he was working for the very gangsters he was hired to arrest, specifically Salvatore "Red" Italiano, one of the most notorious Tampa gangsters of that era.

Velasco worked as a "peephole man" for Italiano's numerous gambling houses. Whenever there was a knock on the door, it was Velasco's job to make sure it was not an uninvited guest, AKA a law enforcement officer not on the take. If it was, he had to stall them long enough to allow all evidence to be hidden or cleared from the building. Some gambling establishments had a man on the outside as well. When law enforcement approached, the outside man, known as a "keyhole man," would stick a wooden match inside the keyhole. When the peephole man saw the match poke through the keyhole, he then led the charge to clear all evidence from the house.

Because Velasco worked in law enforcement, he had further value to Italiano. He could shut down any illegal establishment that was not paying protection money to Italiano. One such establishment was the Yellow Shack Café, a popular café on the corner of Sixth Avenue and 10th Street that doubled as a casino when the sun went down. The café's proprietor was Florentino Martinez.

Martinez was a well-beloved Ybor City resident known for his green eyes, well-cropped black hair, collection of fedoras and sharp suits, love for games of chance and for surviving a 1912 attempt on his life at the hands of Robert Anderson, the African-American serial killer who was terrorizing Ybor City that year. He was most beloved, though, for being a true Ybor City rags-to-riches story.

Martinez' mother was from Havana, Cuba. His father was born in the Canary Islands and later made his way to Cuba where he met and married his wife. They then immigrated to Ybor City to work in the cigar factories.

Martinez was born in 1893. Five years later his father died at the Port of Tampa of food poisoning from tainted meat while waiting to embark to Cuba to fight for Cuba's freedom in the Spanish-American War. Over half his unit met the same fate.

Being raised by a single parent meant Martinez became the man of the house and he entered the workforce while still a boy. His careers included cigar maker, carpenter, mechanic, chauffeur and hat salesman. He was always working multiple jobs in order to support his mother and later both his mother and his wife and child. He was able to save a great deal of money as well and used it to open the Yellow Shack Café at some point in the 1920s. It was an instant success. His looks and outgoing personality were enough of a reason for people to flock to the café. When he added the nightlife component of alcohol and gambling, it turned him from an Ybor City everyman to a member of Ybor City's elite; he was raking in the cash. It also landed him smack dab in the middle of the budding Ybor City gang wars. Which crime boss backed him is unknown, but it was obviously not Red Italiano, as proven by the fact that Velasco made the Yellow Shack one of his primary targets for raids.

The raids were not successful in terms of law enforcement; Martinez was never charged with a heavy enough crime to warrant significant jail time. However, in terms of Tampa's underworld, the raids did their job. Patrons tired of the constant law enforcement harassment and decided to stay away from the café. The Yellow Shack went out of business and, overnight, Martinez went from wealthy to down on his luck. He returned to the mechanics trade and to life as an everyman, as another face in the crowd.

Angry, Martinez swore revenge on Velasco. Unfortunately, revenge could have paid a BIG price. Velasco, after all, was a law enforcement official. As remains the case today, touching an officer of the law was followed by a long jail sentence.

Then, a few months after the Yellow Shack was shut down, Velasco was let go by the Hillsborough County Sheriff's Office. It is undocumented why he was fired, but it would not be a stretch to guess that his ties to the underworld were the cause. Velasco was no longer untouchable. He was open territory.

Martinez did not hide his glee. Whenever he saw Velasco about town, he would hurl insults at him, rubbing it in that he too was out of steady work. "You're in the same fix as I am now," he was frequently heard yelling at Velasco.

Their animosity came to blows in the Imperial Café in Ybor City with Velasco coming out of the altercation badly beaten. A short time later, Velasco got his revenge by paying a former police officer to beat Martinez with a blackjack.

Finally, it all came to a head on August 14, 1928.

Martinez had been in an ornery mood all day, challenging anyone in Ybor City to a fight who thought they could take him. Shortly after sundown, a patron at a café into which Martinez staggered took him up on the offer. Angry words were shouted. Chests were poked. And, before any fists were thrown, Martinez' opponent realized he was overmatched. Hoping to scare Martinez, he fired a gun. It worked. Martinez backed away. Law enforcement must have been in the vicinity because both men were arrested almost immediately after the gunshot rung throughout Ybor City. Martinez was charged with disturbing the peace. His opponent was charged with disturbing the peace and discharging a firearm. They were then both released back into the wild Ybor City night.

Slightly before 9 p.m., Martinez arrived at El Dorado Café with Armado Cordoso, Jose Gomez, and Gomez' two daughters. Martinez sat at a table game but before he could make a bet Velasco entered the café. Heated words were immediately exchanged. Velasco decided to leave the gambling room and walked through a door leading to the front room. A few minutes later Martinez and a friend left, exiting through the same door Velasco had used.

BOOM! A lone gunshot was fired.

Moments later, a wounded Martinez was dragged from the building and laid on the sidewalk. As the crowd formed around him, Velasco slipped out the backdoor of the café and nonchalantly walked to Pote's Café around the corner. Martinez made his way to the clinic. An hour later the police were called and they began interviewing potential witnesses. Everyone began following protocol and said they had not seen a thing. Then, someone broke protocol and said they witnessed the entire event. Armado Cordoso actually stood up for his friend and told investigators that Velasco shot Martinez in cold blood.

Velasco was arrested at his home at 4 a.m. He never denied shooting Martinez, but claimed he did so in self-defense. He showed investigators a rip in the chest area of the shirt he'd worn to the café and said it was a result of Martinez trying to stab him in the heart.

Two hours later, Martinez died on the operating table. On August 16, 1928, he was buried in Tampa's Rose Hill Cemetery.

Following the burial, skeletons of the murder began to creep out of the closet. Some of the patrons who were at the café on the night of the murder began anonymously whispering that Martinez did not have a weapon on him that night. Others questioned how Velasco's shirt did not have any blood on it if Martinez attacked him with a knife. He did not even have a scratch on his chest. Velasco was not wearing a baggy shirt that night. It did not seem possible to cut the shirt and not hit skin.

Then, on August 17, 1928, investigators announced that after they completed an autopsy of Martinez' body they believed that a second man held Martinez while he was shot in the abdomen at close range. Who was the other man? Was it the same man who led Martinez from the gambling room? Perhaps Cordoso would expose this second man in court, people wondered.

A preliminary hearing was held on August 18 and a number of witnesses testified that Velasco was at El Dorado and left after the gunshot was heard but no one testified that they saw Velasco fire the gun or that the gun was fired at the café. The court could force people to appear in court as witnesses but they could not force them to admit that they saw anything. It didn't matter, though. As long as Cordoso told the court what he told investigators, Velasco would be convicted. Unfortunately, Cordoso never showed for court. The hearing had to be suspended until the state attorney's lead witness was found.

On August 21, Velasco was released on a $10,000 bond.

On August 24, Cordoso was found in Jacksonville. He was arrested and charged with contempt for ignoring a summons to appear in court. Law enforcement officials brought him back to Tampa and placed him in county jail. When asked why he skipped town, he told investigators that on the morning of the preliminary hearing he was picked up by four men who threatened him, demanding that he leave Tampa and telling him not to testify.

The preliminary hearing was rescheduled for September 28, 1928. Velasco's attorney was C. Jay Hardee and he was "coached" by George "Saturday" Zarate, a well-known gambling head honcho in Tampa, whose rap sheet would later include ballot box stuffing and drug trafficking. He was a bit of a chameleon in Tampa's underworld, affiliated with both the Sicilian mafia and the

Anglo faction led by the Charlie Wall. Zarate was also the owner of Pote's Café.

Zarate interrupted the proceedings on one occasion to correct Cordoso's interpreter and was warned by the judge to "tell Mr. Hardee about it and let him make the objection."

Zarate was obviously not present to coach Velasco. He was there to further intimidate Cordoso from telling the court what he saw. It worked. Though on the night of the murder Cordoso told investigators he saw Velasco shoot Martinez, he told the court that investigators misunderstood him. He testified that he never saw a thing. He said he only heard that Velasco shot Martinez from others in El Dorado in the moments following the gunshot. When the state attorney asked Cordoso about his claim of being threatened to leave Tampa on the morning he was supposed to testify in August, Cordoso stated that he only told investigators that because he thought it would keep him out of jail. He said that he was never told to leave town.

Without a witness who could testify that Velasco shot Martinez in cold blood and not self-defense, the judge was forced to discharge Velasco because of insufficient evidence.

Years later, Velasco's brother, Jimmy, became one of the most powerful men in Tampa's underworld by rigging elections to help his candidates win. Once his candidate was in office, those illegal establishments that paid protection money to the Velasco brothers—Jimmy, Johnny, Arturo and Roy—would be allowed to operate without trouble from law enforcement. In the late 1940s, the Velasco brothers were involved in a failed attempt to assassinate Santo Trafficante Sr., Red Italiano and a host of public officials. This was their move to become the head family in Tampa's underworld. Following the failure, Roy fled to Puerto Rico and became a successful bar owner.

Today, the murder of Florentino Martinez is still considered unsolved, as are a host of other murders that took place during this bloody period in Ybor City's history.

Standard protocol. No one ever saw a thing.

However, in the ensuing years, a new law enforcement team found ways to see everything.

Chapter 6
Tales from the Vice Squad

Originally published in Cigar City Magazine Issue 29 in 2010

March 22, 1958

The sound of urine pinging into a tin bucket echoed throughout the decrepit Ybor City warehouse filled with crates of food destined for Tampa-based restaurants. A few drops splashed from the bucket and, when mixed with the layers of dirt and dust, caked to the floor like an au naturel carpet, beaded into tiny muddy clumps.

Buddy Meisch, a young hard-nosed ex-Tampa cop turned deputy who had been with the Hillsborough County Sheriff's Office Vice Squad for a little over one year, finished his manly duty, zipped up and walked back to the "comfortable chair" he had been lounging on for over 10 hours- a splintered crate containing canned beans. He grabbed his binoculars and stared at his target located 100 yards away; it was the Ybor City home of one of Tampa's most notorious gangsters, Frank Diecidue, the underboss of the Santo Trafficante-led crime ring that controlled the city's underworld.

Meisch's radio squawked, "Homerun." That was the signal for which he had been waiting. He looked back to the target home. Numerous law enforcement officers, guns at the ready, began to creep towards the house, some to the back door, some to the front, others surrounding it. The head of the raid stood before the front door and casually knocked.

History was about to be made. The evidence was inside that home: thousands of *bolita* tickets collected throughout multiple counties- enough to deliver a crippling financial blow to the Trafficante empire and, perhaps, finally a charge that could stick to Santo Trafficante and put him in jail for a long time. The months-long investigation was about to come to fruition.

As if on cue, a rat scurried across the floor of the warehouse. Ironic, thought Meisch; this entire raid was due to rats in the mafia, and the Vice Squad had to plan the raid knowing that rats in the Sheriff's Office could have compromised it at any moment.

Early 1950s

Captain Ellis Clifton didn't know the definition of fear. Perhaps because it often seemed he had an angel on his shoulder as, no matter how dangerous his job became, he never suffered any consequences.

He had been head of the Vice Squad- the Hillsborough County Sheriff's Office's department charged with bringing down the Tampa mafia- since 1953 and had survived his fair share of threats. Thousands of dollars in bounties had been put on his head, yet no one dared to collect. He had been followed by gangsters as though they were the police and he was the criminal, yet nothing ever came of the pursuits. And he had raided dozens of *bolita* parlors and walked away from each unscathed; not a scratch. Yet, in the early 1950s, when he sat in his car parked on a desolate road in the middle of Tampa's "boondocks," a known Sicilian felon seated next to him, he was shaking. The shakes were not from fear, though, but from excitement.

Just a few days earlier, Clifton busted the Sicilian committing a crime. But, rather than arresting him, he made a deal. If the Sicilian would meet him on a desolate road at a specific time in a few days' time and tell him everything he knew about Tampa's underworld, he would let him go. The known felon agreed. He provided Clifton with a "family tree," a who's who in the Tampa underworld, as well as an understanding of how the gambling operations were run.

"I finally got a guy who was a Sicilian and I told him I would lay off him if he would talk to me for six months," explained Clifton. "So I got me a legal pad and got him in the car with me and we talked for five hours." Clifton would never reveal the source, though. Not even over 50 years later when he knew he would soon succumb to cancer.

As the Sicilian felon bared his soul, Clifton understood why it had been so difficult to make any major headway in the Sheriff's Office's war on *bolita*. Sure they had made dozens of small *bolita* busts, but nothing earth shattering. They were never able to find where a major haul of *bolita* tickets or money was counted. The reason: the Sicilians knew what they were doing. The tickets and money for major *bolita* rings were each separately run through a maze of bureaucracy and multiple hand-offs until they reached their final destinations, making them hard to follow unless law enforcement had inside information.

According to Clifton's new Sicilian source, the maze started with the street peddlers, who were also called "writers." Some of the street peddlers literally sold numbers on the street corners, while others may have sold numbers from an establishment they owned- restaurant, café, bar, hardware store, etc. Once the player made his bet, the peddler gave the player a ticket with the number he played printed on it. The peddler then called a "Call-In House" and read the "Call-In Guy" the numbers he sold and to whom and the Call-In Guy would write up tickets for each sale for his records. The peddler rarely knew who the Call-In Guy was; he simply knew what phone number to call.

Tampa bolita numbers were originally thrown in the city; 100 numbered balls were placed in a sack and the winning numbers were pulled. By the 1950s, however, the major bolita games used that week's winning Cuban lottery numbers, which were drawn in Cuba at noon on Saturdays. Everyone involved in bolita in Tampa- from the players on up- listened to a Cuban radio station at noon for the winning numbers. At 12:01 p.m., the Call-In Guy would gather all his *bolita* tickets, place them in an envelope, and walk to a specific street and look for a specific car. When the car slowly drove by, the Call-In Guy nonchalantly handed the driver (D1) his envelope. The Call-In Guy's job was done for the day and he had no idea where the driver was going.

D1 collected from all the Call-In Guys in a specific territory. Once he had collected from all his Call-In Guys, he then drove down a specific street and looked for a specific car. When the two cars cruised by one another, D1 handed his envelopes to the other driver (D2). D1's job was done for the day and he had no idea where D2 was going.

The process repeated itself another five to eight times in each territory, each driver handing his envelope to another driver, never knowing where the new driver was going. The only driver who knew the final destination of the envelope was the last driver, who then took the envelope to the "Drop House," where *bolita* tickets from numerous Call-In Houses and dozens of peddlers were delivered and calculated. The money went through the exact process, but was taken to another house. The tickets and money were always kept separate, so that if one was busted the other was safe.

Clifton's Sicilian source helped him to begin to crack the mazes and also provided him with names and addresses of numerous *bolita* dealers. Meanwhile, the family tree helped Clifton identify the major players in town.

"Ellis was everywhere," said Meisch. "[The bolita dealers] called him the rabbit because he was always popping up all over town."

"One Saturday, Charlie Whitt [a third partner] and I and Ellis went to a local grocery store in Ybor City–I can't remember which one–because we knew they were selling *bolita* [and knew it was also a Call-In House]. The numbers were called in at 12 p.m., so we'd wait until 12:01 p.m. to make a bust because we knew the *bolita* tickets would be scattered on a table so the numbers could be tallied. We went to the store and we went up to the front door and an old man was coming out and when he saw us he hollered, 'Tres conejos.' We went in and the old man who owned that grocery story was scrambling to get rid of his *bolita* tickets. Well, we came to realize that *tres* is three and *conejo* is rabbit. So the old man yelled 'the three rabbits', tipping them off that we were coming in. So, I guess after a while we were referred to as the three rabbits."

The Vice Squad often cut deals with those they arrested for information in exchange for less jail time or none at all. If the prospect of jail time didn't scare them, the Vice Squad would bribe the answers out of them. The Sheriff's Office had a fund they called "The Emergency Fund" that was earmarked for such bribery. If the peddler or driver gave them information that led to a small *bolita* raid, they were paid a few dollars. But, if it turned into a major raid, they'd be paid $200–a lot of money for a nickel and dime *bolita* peddler or driver to earn in the 1950s.

The more information they received, the more frequent the busts became. "It seemed like we were busting somebody on gambling charges every Saturday," said Whitt. And with each *bolita* bust, the Vice Squad gathered more information that led to more and larger busts.

Usually, a peddler would provide Clifton with the Call-In House number. Clifton and his men would track down the owner of the phone number and stake out the establishment. When the Call-In Guy would leave to deliver his tickets to a driver, Clifton and his crew would follow him and begin tracking the maze of exchanges. Once the maze was documented, they'd return the following week to arrest everyone who was part of it. The arrests had to be quick and well planned, though.

"The *bolita* numbers were often printed on cigarette paper," explained Whitt. "That paper was easily flammable and would burn quickly if the cops walked in ."

Despite all this activity, after months of arrests, a $200 reward for a huge bust had yet to be paid. Some of the *bolita* busts were substantial, but none were major. Then, in early 1958, Clifton found himself yet another informant looking to earn a few dollars, and the new informant provided him with information that while worth $200, was in fact priceless. The informant told Clifton specifics about a maze of *bolita* tickets that began in St. Petersburg every week and included *bolita* tickets for Hillsborough, Pinellas, Manatee and Polk counties. This was the biggest *bolita* maze Clifton had been tipped off on. The next Saturday, Clifton got to work.

Following an entire *bolita* maze was tough; a typical *bolita* maze wound through Tampa Bay for miles. To follow the drivers and not be seen was no easy task. Plus, when following at a distance, it was easy to lose the drivers. To compound matters, this particular *bolita* maze began in St. Petersburg. But, Clifton had heard that another Sheriff's Office in the state of Florida had recently used an airplane for surveillance and decided to mimic their tactic.

Clifton hovered a few hundred feet above the route in a tiny airplane. Because this was only the second time in the history of the state that an airplane had tailed criminals, Clifton had nothing to worry about. The drivers and peddlers had no reason to believe that an airplane was following them. He was able to document the entire route, all the way to the Drop House.

The Drop House he found was the residence of Frank Diecidue, who, according to Clifton's original informant, was THE underboss of the Trafficante crime family- Santo's number one *bolita* man in Tampa. This was BIG.

Despite the huge discovery, Clifton kept the news to himself for a few weeks. He was always careful with his information. Rats were everywhere.

"You couldn't park a car in Ybor City without somebody being alert," said Clifton.

"We always had to watch our backs and go home at night and make sure we had plenty of ammunition, if you understand what I am saying," said Whitt.

"I remember when I first went to work for the Vice Squad, they told me that morning that by the evening time the bolita people would know who I was, my car, my tag number, where I lived and my phone number," said Meisch. "I got home that evening around 9:30 p.m., the phone rang, and when I answered it they hung up. It was them. For sure, they knew right away."

Mob informants were also located within the Sheriff's Office. The late-Roland Manteiga, former publisher of *La Gaceta* newspaper who had his own inside sources at the Sheriff's Office, wrote in March 1958 that Clifton and the Vice Squad spoke via radio on private radio waves rather than over the designated Sheriff's Office radio waves because they didn't know who they could trust within their own ranks.

Clifton trusted his two Vice Squad partners--Meisch and Whitt--but, before he told them, he watched Diecidue's house for a few more weeks, just to be certain that it wasn't a onetime Drop House. He didn't want to get their hopes up until he was sure it was the regular Drop House. Once he was sure, he told his partners and they began to plan their raid.

Everyone involved in the raid was told to drive to St. Petersburg at various times, so as not to draw any suspicion. They then all met in a hotel, went over the plans, and returned to Tampa, again at various times.

Meisch was one of the first to return to Tampa. He and another officer were charged with surveillance from a warehouse 100 yards away from Diecidue's home. They were given coffee, some snacks and a bucket to use as a toilet; they had no reason to leave that warehouse. They were to have a pair of eyes on that home from 5:30 a.m. Saturday morning until the raid began in the late afternoon. If anything out of the ordinary took place, they were ordered to inform Clifton.

Clifton then set up men at every exchange point along the route. When each exchange was made, the particular officer radioed in the news via code words. The chosen code was baseball. When the first exchange was made, an officer radioed in, "The ball game has started." When the second was made, an officer radioed in, "The batter is coming up," the third officer said, "He is on first base," and so on. Eight exchanges had eight different baseball phrases, with the final delivery to Diecidue's being, "Home run."

Clifton, a former newspaper reporter, knew this raid was going to be huge, so that morning he called a friend who worked with a local television station and tipped him off, allowing a camera crew to be there with him when they broke down the door.

Around 3:50 p.m., the raid began.

Clifton went to the front door with the camera crew and some backup officers. Whitt and some additional officers went to the back door to make sure no one could escape and more backup officers surrounded the house.

When Clifton knocked, Diecidue's wife, Rose, looked outside, saw the small army of law enforcement officers on her lawn, and asked what they wanted, to which Clifton replied that if she didn't open the door they would force it open. She refused to open it, so Clifton ordered Whitt and his officers to force open the back door using a fire axe. Once inside, Clifton and his crew arrested Biaggio

Savrino, Frank Ippolito, Rose Diecidue, Alice Lazzara and Primo Lazzara. Upon searching the home, all the law enforcement agents were blown away by what they found. They knew this raid would be big, but not this big.

They found thousands of *bolita* tickets hidden throughout the house–the most Clifton had ever seen in one place–adding up to tens of thousands of dollars. More importantly, they found the names of 50–100 individuals involved in that particular *bolita* ring–a ring that was estimated to earn millions of dollars a year. This was one of the largest bolita raids ever on the west coast of Florida. The only thing missing from the house was the key man; Frank Diecidue was nowhere to be found. But, this was his home. Clifton knew he had him so he waited.

Following the raid, the television crew's footage was broadcast on the evening news, so Diecidue must have known about it. He didn't run, though. Instead, he returned to his home and was peacefully arrested.

Diecidue was convicted of running an illegal lottery, but the other defendants were freed after mistrials. Despite convicting only one individual, this raid was considered a resounding success, as the list of individuals involved in *bolita* led to numerous raids throughout the Tampa Bay area in the ensuing weeks. However, none of those raids included or led to the arrest of Santo Trafficante, Jr., who was safely living in Cuba where law enforcement could not touch him. He was the man the Vice Squad wanted. Unknown to the other members of the Vice Squad, however, was that Clifton already had a plan in place to snag Tampa's most wanted man.

Chapter 7
Sleeping With the Enemy

Originally published in Cigar City Magazine Issue 28 in 2010

For over half a century, Captain Ellis Clifton kept a secret about the Hillsborough County Sheriff's Office. He didn't tell the author who based a book on his career spent battling organized crime in Tampa. He didn't tell his partners in the Hillsborough County Vice Squad. He didn't tell his family.

Then, in 2007, at the age of 80, while sitting in a wheelchair on a dock outside his Florida vacation home, an oxygen tank at the ready, knowing he had just a few months of life left, he nonchalantly told me his secret, and he told me on film.

"So we made a deal with Castro up in the hills," he said, taking a brief pause to catch his breath. "If we helped run him guns, he would send us those guys."

By "we" he meant the Hillsborough County Sheriff's Office. "Those guys" were Santo Trafficante, Jr. and his crew, who ran their Tampa crime syndicate from the comfort of legal casinos in Fulgencio Batista-led Cuba in the 1950s.

We're not talking about a crazy conspiracy theorist making a controversial statement. This was Captain Ellis Clifton, head of the Hillsborough County Vice Squad, the department that was charged with bringing down the Tampa mafia and ending Tampa's "Era of Blood." The Tampa mafia considered Ellis Clifton to be the most dangerous law enforcement officer in Tampa and his secret deal with Fidel Castro is a perfect example as to why he was so feared. He would do almost anything to bring the criminals to justice.

What were the specifics of his deal? He never said.

My brother Pete and I interviewed him for our documentary on infamous Tampa gangster Charlie Wall. While on film, he mentioned the deal nonchalantly, as though this half-century-old secret was the equivalent of a secret family recipe, not a revelation that implicated one of the largest law enforcement agencies in the state of Florida with illegal arms dealings with foreign entities seeking to overthrow a sovereign government. He continued on with his fascinating tales of investigating the Tampa mafia and his off-the-cuff statement temporarily took a back seat as I listened to his stories, mesmerized by the exciting life he had led.

When Clifton needed a break and the camera was off, I had time to contemplate all that he had said. His fleeting comments regarding secret dealings with Fidel Castro echoed in my thoughts. I wanted to know more. Before we began filming again, I asked if we could focus on his deal with Castro. He huffed, smiled slyly, and, in his smooth Florida Cracker drawl, said, "Some things should go with me to my grave."

A few months later, he passed away, succumbing to throat cancer, leaving a wife, four adult children and numerous questions about his historic deal with Castro behind.

The first question being: Could he have lied to me?

"No. Not at all," wrote Ace Atkins in an email to me when asked if Clifton was the type of man who lied. Atkins is the author of White Shadow, a fictional crime drama based on the real life 1955 murder of Charlie Wall. Clifton was the lead investigator on the murder case and was one of Atkin's top sources while doing research for the book. The two became close friends.

"[Ellis Clifton] was a straight shooter," stressed Atkins. "He was not the type of man to lie."

Atkins suggested that the manner in which Clifton got his start in law enforcement says everything you need to know about his honesty.

Prior to joining the Hillsborough County Sheriff's Office, Clifton was a crime beat reporter for the *Tampa Tribune*. On the evening of the Gasparilla Parade in 1953, one of his informants told him that a high stakes illegal gambling game was taking place in a room in the Tampa Terrace Hotel in downtown Tampa. Clifton fearlessly went by to check it out and discovered that some of his bosses from the *Tribune* were already there. They weren't investigating the illegal gambling for a story, though. They were gambling. Clifton's wife was seven months pregnant and he knew that calling the police would cost him his job and leave him and his wife in a financial bind. Despite the potential ramifications, Clifton felt he had to do the right thing. He left the makeshift gambling parlor and called the Sheriff's Office, but by the time they arrived someone had tipped off the gamblers. When the officers arrived, there was no sign of any illegal activity. When Clifton went to work the next day, he was fired. However, that same day, Hillsborough County Sheriff Ed Blackburn called Clifton and offered him a job.

"Blackburn won the sheriff's election by promising to clean up the illegal gambling," explained Clifton.

The Hillsborough County Sheriff's Office did not have the best reputation. Its previous sheriff, Hugh Culbreath, was exposed as corrupt by the Kefauver Committee. Sheriff Culbreath was implicated by a number of individuals for being in cahoots with Tampa's crime syndicate.

"Human life in Tampa was almost as cheap as the sand of the beach," wrote Estes Kefauver, the senator who led the nationwide investigation. "In nineteen years there have been fourteen murders and six attempted assassinations in the Tampa underworld- and only one conviction ... The moral of the Tampa story is this: if good citizens of a community shut their eyes to wholesale violation of a law- even if it is a law prohibiting something that a lot of people happen to like- law enforcement and honesty in public office will go to hell in a handcart."

To clean up the Sheriff's Office, Sheriff Blackburn needed honest men, and Clifton was tapped as one of those honest men. Despite having zero law enforcement experience, he was placed on the Vice Squad; Blackburn saw him as a man who could not be bought off by organized crime.

Given his background, it would seem odd for a man with such a strong reputation for honesty to suddenly begin lying in his final days and risk destroying his legacy. He had nothing to gain by telling a lie. He was already a legendary law enforcement officer and he was not getting paid for the interview.

However, prior to our 2007 interview, Clifton had never told anyone of his deal with Castro. Why?

Atkins spoke with Clifton about his days with the Vice Squad for hundreds of hours, yet he never mentioned his deal with Castro. Nor did he ever mention this deal to anyone in his family. And neither of his two ex-Vice Squad partners- Charlie Whitt and Buddy Meische- had ever heard of it. Yet, according to his son and one of his ex-partners, that does not mean it didn't happen.

"It is both possible and probable that he was part of a deal with Castro to hand over Santo Trafficante," said Clifton's son, David. "He had an amazing way with people. He could get them to talk and drop their guard, which always lent itself to him making some amazing contacts and getting information."

This ability enabled Clifton to put together the first "mafia family tree" in the history of the state of Florida, an outline of how the mafia was organized, from the lowest street thugs to the top brass. "It was a bibliography," explained Clifton during our 2007 interview. "I had more information than anyone."

Who gave him this information? He never revealed his source.

"Ellis always had good information and good contacts," said Charlie Whitt. "He would inform us that he knew where a big *bolita* house was and he'd plan the raid, but he would never tell us how he learned this information. He just seemed to know everything and everyone."

If he never shared his sources with his partners, it's doubtful he would have told them about his deal with Castro. And, there was a window of opportunity for the two to broker a deal.

In November 1955, Fidel Castro came to Tampa to found a branch of his revolutionary army, "The 26th of July Movement," and to raise money for his revolution against Cuba's then-president Fulgencio Batista. So, it is possible that an undocumented and secret meeting between Clifton and Castro took place during Castro's 1955 Tampa visit; a meeting Clifton never told his partners about, a meeting at which a deal was struck. Or, perhaps Clifton later made the deal through one of Tampa's 26th of July members, who had direct contact with Castro while he was fighting Batista from the mountains of Cuba.

But why would Clifton make such a deal?

Fidel Castro (standing to the left of the man holding a picture of Jose Marti) visits the home of July 26th organizers at a home in Ybor City in 1955.

One of the many reasons Castro said Batista needed to be overthrown was his cozy relationship with American organized crime families, who ran numerous casinos in Cuba. In Castro's view, the casinos, which were legal under Batista, brought rampant alcohol abuse and gambling to the island, and acted as a cover for illegal drugs and sex trafficking. Under Batista, Castro argued, Cuba became a safe haven for mafia leaders who could run their illegal operations in the United States without worrying about the prying eyes and ears of U.S. law enforcement officials. Enough mobsters made Cuba their regular home or vacation spot that it became known as "The Mafia's Playground."

One of the top casino owners was Tampa mafia boss Santo Trafficante, Jr., a man both Clifton and Castro wanted out of Cuba.

Despite knowing that without a shadow of a doubt Trafficante was the top dog in Tampa's underworld, the Sheriff's Office couldn't charge Trafficante with anything because there was no direct evidence linking him to anything illegal.

"[Trafficante] ran all his crime out of Cuba," said Clifton, explaining that as long as Trafficante was allowed to stay in Cuba, there was too much open water and too many people in between him and the people he did business with for the Hillsborough County Sheriff's Office to build a case. If Clifton was going to bust Trafficante, he needed to get him out of Cuba.

It w as a fter e xplaining t he d ifficulties o f b ringing charges against Trafficante that Clifton made the following s tatement while my b rother's camera rolled:

"So we made a deal with Castro up in the hills. If we helped run guns to him, he would send us those guys."

Throughout the Cuban Revolution, numerous gun smuggling operations had ties to Tampa.

In 1957, the Philomar III, a yacht loaded with arms and military uniforms that were to be delivered to Castro's revolutionary army, was seized by U.S. agents off the Florida Keys. The yacht was purchased in Tampa.

In 1958, another yacht, The Harpoon, loaded with arms, was s eized at Port Everglades, F lorida. Four Cubans who lived i n Tampa were among the 33 arrested.

Also in 1958, a s mall v essel p acked with a rms, El Orion, was s eized o ff the lower Texas Gulf Coast. Among the 36 Cubans arrested were t hree Cubans from T ampa.

Except for Victoriano Manteiga, f ounder o f *La Gaceta newspaper* and founding president of Tampa's 26th of July Movement, no Tampa reporter knew more about Castro's r evolution t han Tom Durkin, who covered the revolution from Cuba as a photojournalist for the *St. Petersburg Times* and *La Gaceta*. According to a Durkin article published in the *St. Petersburg Times* on January 9, 1959, "One U.S. sympathizer even offered to provide the rebels a small submarine for sneaking weapons to Castro. His offer was rejected by the cautious Ybor group 'because w e d idn't k now w here i t c ame fro m.' ... Admitted by Ybor Castro supporters, but a nonymously, is t he fact t hat 150 machine g uns seized in Miami last year, packed in oil drums, passed through Tampa … An obsolete U.S. bomber, seized at Fort Lauderdale as weapons were being loaded, originated its flight in Tampa. Among those arrested were four *Tampans* from Ybor City."

Did Clifton and the Sheriff's Office directly provide Castro or Castro's Tampa-based revolutionaries with guns? Or, perhaps they helped introduce the Tampa revolutionaries to gun dealers. Or, maybe Durkin provided the best clue as to what the deal could have been when he wrote in his 1959 article, "Despite all the activity in Tampa, Tampa Customs and Border Patrol officials report no actual arms seizures in this area."

Perhaps Clifton and the Sheriff's Office simply agreed to look the other way. Considering the number of informants and snitches Clifton said he and the Sheriff's Office had, it is hard to believe that law enforcement would have no knowledge of the numerous arms shipments originating or passing through Tampa. But, with Clifton gone, we'll never really know the answer.

Clifton did explain, however, that Castro did live up to his end of the bargain.

When Batista fled Cuba on January 1, 1959, numerous mafia bosses who ran casinos in Cuba also fled the island. Castro repeatedly stated throughout the revolution that when he overthrew Batista he would shut down the casinos and imprison any criminals that remained in Cuba. Some gangsters fled so quickly they left behind millions of dollars in cash. Trafficante stayed in Cuba.

Some historians have noted that Trafficante contributed money to Castro's revolution, believing Castro would allow him to continue to run his casinos. Other historians have written that Trafficante believed Castro would come around once he realized how much money the casinos generated. Others claim he stayed in Cuba because the New York City District Attorney's Office was investigating Trafficante for the murder of Albert Anastasia, the boss of what would later become known as the Gambino crime family.

When Castro learned that Trafficante was still in Cuba, he had him arrested, imprisoned and slated for execution.

Victoriano Manteiga, who was a friend of both Trafficante and Castro's, called Castro personally and pleaded with him to release Trafficante, but failed. A handful of Tampa Cubans also made a trip to Cuba to try and free Trafficante, but they too failed.

Trafficante's attorney, Frank Ragano, wrote in his book, Mob Lawyer, that he brokered the deal for Trafficante's release. Not so, said Clifton, who claimed that Trafficante brokered his own release and that the Cuban government arranged for Clifton to pick up Trafficante from the airport on August 18, 1959.

"I cut a deal with a Cuban official from National Airlines and another with the Immigration Department. [The Sheriff's Office] had [contact with] a man who was chief of the Cuban Air Force, and the sergeant in my department talked to him at least once a week to find out Santo's status and when he was getting out," explained Clifton. "So one night, around 12:30 a.m., I got a phone call from National Airlines and the Immigration Department saying they had put Trafficante on a plane and he would be landing in Florida soon."

Clifton instructed the Cubans to detain Trafficante until he arrived, armed with a New York County District Attorney Office subpoena from the Anastasia murder case.

When Clifton arrived, he said Trafficante "wasn't dressed all natty like he normally was. His pants were short to the top of his shoes. His cuffs were also short and he had on a real ratty shirt and shoes. [It looked like they dressed him in] something they found in the corner. It looked like they dressed him as poor as they could to make him look bad. I barely recognized him. I looked him up and down and said, 'I am Captain Clifton with the Hillsborough County Sheriff's Office,' and he said, 'Clifton, you son of a bitch, you've been hounding my ass ever since I first saw you as a reporter.' I let him rave on and on, but I said, 'The bottom line is, if you show your face on the street, we have a court order to arrest you every time we see you.' Well, he raved on for a bit again and we chatted back and forth and I said, 'I won't arrest you today. I'll let you go,' [because] his attorney wasn't there, contrary to [Ragano's] book and all his bullshit. [Ragano] didn't help get the guy at all. Santo said so! So as I started out the door, I looked back to Santo and asked him, 'How'd you get out.' And he said, 'I gave him $3 million and they let me save $600,000; that's all they left me with. That's why I stayed so long, because I wouldn't give them the money and they only kept me alive because they wanted the money. They're bigger crooks than we are.'"

In the morning, Clifton said he learned that the New York County District Attorney's Office had cancelled the subpoena from the Anastasia investigation. Ragano then went down to the Hillsborough County Courthouse and filed a writ of habeas corpus, claiming Clifton and the Hillsborough County Sheriff's Office were harassing Trafficante. Clifton said the court order meant he could not arrest Trafficante.

"But it wasn't in the law that I couldn't follow him from 300 feet away. So I put a 24-hour tail on him," said Clifton. "If he went to the Columbia [Restaurant], I had two or three men on him. If he went home, I had men on him. He couldn't go anywhere and conduct business under that kind of environment."

Clifton said that, in time, Trafficante tired of the constant surveillance, not only because it took away his privacy, but also because he couldn't run his criminal organization with police nearby at all times. So, Clifton explained, Trafficante began spending most of his time in Miami. And, most importantly, he explained, without Cuba as a safe haven, Trafficante's criminal organization began to lose power.

Ellis Clifton and Ace Atkins at King Corona in Ybor City, Florida.

A week prior to interviewing Clifton for the Charlie Wall Documentary, my brother and I joined him and Ace Atkins for beers at King Corona in Ybor City. Before Clifton allowed us to film his stories, he wanted to get to know us. After about two beers and an hour of conversation, he warmed to us and began to open his vault a bit, explaining to us that no matter what anyone thinks of Castro's politics, he was one of the most important factors that led to the downfall of the American M afia, a s m ob leaders i n cities a cross t he n ation found it as impossible as Trafficante did to run their criminal organizations in the same manner as they did in Cuba.

The details of the Sheriff's Office's deal with Castro may never be known. But, whatever the deal was, it worked. You may not agree with the tactic, but it was effective. It helped weaken the grip organized crime had on Tampa.

While Clifton's deal with Castro made his life easier, another Tampa man's deal with Castro made his life hell, turning him into a man without a country.

Chapter 8
The Odyssey of Carlos Carbonell

Originally published in Cigar City Magazine Issue 31 in 2010

The l ife o f C uban n ative C arlos C arbonell fell apart following Fidel Castro's successful coup toppling Cuban dictator Fulgencio Batista.

His home was vandalized. He and his oldest son were fired from their jobs and his youngest son was thrown off his baseball team. Some of his friends were physically assaulted. His life was under constant threat—and all of this was due to his political beliefs.

In late 1960, tired of living in fear, he decided to escape the country that was oppressing him and move to a country that would accept his political beliefs; Carlos Carbonell escaped the United States and moved to the Castro-led Cuba.

Yes. You read that correctly. He fled the United States for Cuba.

Carlos was a founding member of Tampa's "26th of July Movement", Castro's revolutionary army. The Tampa branch supported Castro throughout the Cuban Revolution and in the months following the victory, sending Castro money, food, clothing, and medical and military supplies. Some of the Batista supporters who fled Cuba following his ousting moved to Tampa and made it their mission to harass those who helped Castro, which included Carlos. The police did not protect Carlos, nor did the government. The only place he believed he would be safe was in Cuba, or so he thought.

The constant counter-revolutionary attacks in Cuba put all Cubans in danger. The sounds of exploding bombs and gun shots were as common at night as dancing and smoking cigars. Then, Castro announced that Cuba would become a Communist nation, which was followed by the Cuban Missile Crisis. Due to the constant threat of a U.S. invasion, life in Cuba became as dangerous if not more dangerous than life in Tampa.

In late 1962, Carlos Carbonell decided it was once again time to relocate due to safety concerns. This time, he would go back to the United States, but the Cuban government would not allow him to leave. He was a former revolutionary and he held a much sought after government job. Such a man leaving Cuba would have been a shout to the world that Castro's government was not working–so he had to sneak out of Cuba. With help from friends within the Cuban police, he snuck aboard a plane, hidden by the cover of the midnight sky, and a few hours later landed in Mexico, where he was granted asylum and reentry to the United States, thus ending the long and fascinating odyssey of Carlos Carbonell.

"All my father ever wanted was to live in a free Cuba," said his youngest son, George Carbonell. "That is why he supported Castro. He just wanted Cuba to be free."

How could supporting Castro free Cuba?

"Cuba was anything but free before Castro won the revolution," said George. "[Fulgencio] Batista was a tyrant."

Carlos Carbonell was born in Havana, Cuba on September 23, 1896. In the 1920s, he moved to Ybor City to work in the cigar factories. In Ybor City, he met and married Isabel Toledo. The couple moved back to Cuba to start a family in the 1930s, where their three children were born–Hector, George and Daisy. Then, in the mid-1940s, they moved back to Tampa.

Carlos did not lose touch with his native country, though. He followed the political s ituation closely through firsthand accounts from family and friends living in Cuba a nd through Ybor City's *La Gaceta* newspaper, which was then primarily a S panish n ewspaper c overing n ews from Spain a nd Cuba, t he crux o f Ybor City's Latin community. W hat h e h eard and read a bout most was t he fear that Batista instilled in the residents of the island nation.

Batista had b een Cuban p resident from 1 940–1944 a nd was running for the office again in 1952. Realizing h e was g oing t o lose the e lection t o Roberto Agramonte, B atista, b acked b y t he Cuban army h e o nce led as general, staged a coup and forcefully s eized the presidency. Batista's reign as "president" of Cuba was a t error-filled time i n Cuba. H e controlled the Cuban p eople through fear. Freedom o f t he p ress a nd s peech w ere o ppressed, a s Batista " dealt w ith" those who spoke against his government.

"I h ad a c ousin who was killed by Batista's police for demonstrating in the street against the way he ran the government," said George.

Batista buddied-up to t he A merican m afia, allowing t hem to purchase controlling i nterest i n C uba's l uxurious h otel and casino industry. American gangsters paid Batista $250,000 under the table to buy into or open a casino, and then had to give him a percentage of the slot machines. In return, the Cuban police turned the other cheek as the g angsters p eddled s ex from t heir e stablishments, turning t he Cuban women into prostitutes s old to tourists. Sugar was the official cash crop of Cuba, but its real moneymakers were alcohol, gambling and sex.

"It was a disgusting time in Cuba's history," said George. "My father was very p olitical, a lways p aying attention to what was going on. He wanted to help his country."

On July 26, 1953, a then-young rebel by the name of Fidel Castro staged an unsuccessful coup in Cuba. Dozens of his revolutionaries were either killed in the coup attempt or tortured to death following their capture. Castro was captured but his life was spared. Instead, he was imprisoned.

During his trial, he gave his famous speech, "History Will Absolve Me," a c all to Cubans a round t he world to fight to f ree C uba from the iron grip of Batista.

While Castro may have failed to overthrow Batista in 1953, he became a living legend among the Cuban men and women both in Cuba and abroad who wanted Batista ousted. Castro was seen as a modern day José Martí, Cuba's most famous freedom fighter, often referred to as the "Apostle of Cuban Independence" and the "Cuban George Washington." Marti's powerful speeches rallied Cubans to free themselves from Spanish rule in the late 1800s.

Carlos Carbonell was among Castro's followers, regularly following his exploits in *La Gaceta*, so when he read in the newspaper that Castro would be visiting Tampa in November 1955, he wanted to meet him and help him with his quest to free Cuba.

"What people need to realize is that the Castro that came to Tampa was not a Communist Castro," explained George. "People may tell you he was, but they were misinformed."

The CIA agrees with George, as Castro's CIA files from 1955 through 1960 state that he was NOT a Communist. The files are public record and easily accessible through the CIA's website if you doubt the claim.

Castro arrived in Tampa on November 23, 1955 and named *La Gaceta* Publisher Victoriano Manteiga as the president of the Tampa branch of the "26th of July Movement." Manteiga then named Carbonell treasurer.

"I was with my father when he first met Castro over at the *La Gaceta* office in Ybor City. I was 13 years old and I had heard so much about Castro that I wanted to ask him if I could go back to Mexico and help him fight," laughed George. "Of course, when I shook his hand I was too scared to ask so I just told him it was nice to meet him."

On November 26, Castro spoke to around 300 Cubans at the CIO Labor Union, located at 1226 E. Seventh Avenue between 12th and 13th streets in Ybor City, the same building that today houses the Marti-Maceo Social Club. He spoke for 30 minutes, invoking more comparisons to Jose Marti by quoting the famous Cuban throughout his speech. He also listed Batista's many atrocities and promised to overthrow the dictator or die trying. At the end of the meeting, $191.02 was raised in support of Castro's revolution.

Castro left Tampa the next day and Tampa's 26th of July Movement continued to stump throughout the city in support of the revolution, asking every

Cuban to donate a portion of their weekly paycheck to the cause. The 26th of July Movement would then send the money, along with clothes, food and medical supplies to Mexico, where Castro returned following his U.S. tour.

In December 1956, Castro and a small army of men returned to Cuba, took refuge in the mountains, and began the fighting phase of the revolution. Meanwhile, the branches of the 26th of July Movement located throughout the United States continued to send money and supplies to Cuba via Mexico. According to George, supplies were no longer limited to food, clothing and medicine—arms were added to the list.

"I remember opening my father's closet and I saw a box. When I opened it, I found two grenades," said George. "I mean, brand spanking new grenades. I picked one up and my father walked in and yelled at me to put it down and to never mess with it again."

Tampa's 26th of July Movement supported the revolution for the next few years. Then, on New Year's Day 1959, the world woke up to the news that Batista had fled Cuba. Castro's revolution had triumphed.

"There was a party held in Ybor City and West Tampa," said George. "Don't let anyone tell you otherwise—Tampa supported Castro at the time. Today, people like to pretend that Tampa did not support Castro. Well, Tampa did. There was a motorcade [on New Year's Day] that went from Ybor City to West Tampa; 50–60 cars long, all waving Cuban flags and "26th of July" flags and sounding their horns as every Cuban they drove by cheered and waved. Batista was gone. Castro had won and everyone was happy."

The proof that Tampa supported Castro is not difficult to locate. Batista and his henchmen depleted the Cuban treasury, stealing hundreds of millions of dollars before fleeing Cuba, leaving the country broke. Tampa's 26th of July Movement collected money that they sent to Cuba to support the new government. *La Gaceta* published weekly lists of those who donated and how much they gave. In West Tampa and Ybor City, Tampa's 26th of July Movement collected thousands of dollars, which was a lot of money for blue collar immigrants to give in 1959.

As a part of Tampa's 26th of July Movement since its inception, Carlos

Carbonell was looked upon as a hero. But, in just a few months' time his world turned upside down, as he went from hero to traitor.

Despite Batista's crimes against the Cuban people, the U.S. government supported him because he sold the U.S. land in Cuba at reduced prices and allowed U.S. businesses to gain monopolies in the sugar industry and in utility companies, lining the pockets of these U.S. businesses, who in return lined the pockets of Batista. When Castro won the revolution, he was a wild card, not a leader who would allow the U.S. to control Cuban interests. Instead, he wanted to free Cuba from what he deemed to be the United States' financial control.

When the revolutionary government came to power, it confiscated properties owned by Batista's collaborators and U.S. citizens and businesses in the name of his Agrarian Reform Program. This program sought to put land back in the hands of the Cuban peasants rather than allowing the U.S. to own all the land—land Castro claimed they purchased at a cheap price from a crooked leader. In retaliation, a few weeks before the end of 1959, U.S. military airplanes dropped incendiary devices to burn the sugar fields, thus reducing the harvest of Cuba's prized crop.

In early 1960, Vice-President Richard Nixon threatened to punish Castro for taking U.S. property in Cuba. These threats including reducing the amount of sugar the U.S. purchased from Cuba, knowing such a move would cripple the Cuban economy. In response, Castro announced a trade agreement with the Soviet Union.

"[Castro] had to side with the Russians to survive," explained George. "They had money, Cuba had none, and the U.S. was not helping him." Once Castro made the trade agreement with the Russians, life turned sour for Carlos Carbonell.

"The trouble came from the Batista people who fled this way," said George Carbonell.

Following Castro's victory, a sword spread that Castro was trying Batista's henchmen in court and putting those guilty of violent crimes to death, Batista's most ardent supporters fled Cuba for the United States, many of whom went to Tampa, where they took out their anger on those who supported Castro.

The headquarters of Tampa's 26th of July Movement in Ybor City was vandalized–windows and furniture were smashed and important documents were stolen. Members' cars were egged and their homes were splashed with red paint to symbolize their affinity for a "Communist" leader, claiming Castro's deal with Russia meant he was Communist. However, it is important to note that, according to the CIA, Castro had not yet embraced Communism. "That's just what people did when they wanted to ruin your name back then," explained George. "They said you were Communist. My father was not a Communist. He never was."

The unluckiest of Tampa's Castro supporters were beaten up; Batista supporters would wait until they had one or two Castro supporters greatly outnumbered then issued their beatings. The Carbonells were never physically assaulted, but their lives were shattered.

Carlos was regularly bothered by the FBI on Tampa's 26th of July Movement activities, hoping to get an insight on Castro's new government by questioning those who supported it.

According to Carlos' FBI file, he was fired from the bakery at which he worked–None Such Bakery–because the owners claimed their customers threatened to cease frequenting their establishment if they did not fire the "Communist" Carlos. To survive, Carlos sold *La Bohemia*–an official Cuban government publication–around Ybor City and West Tampa. He received the magazine once a week from Cuba, paid the freight on the magazine and then sold it to newsstands for 27 cents a copy. In turn it was sold for 38 cents. According to Carlos' FBI file, he told the FBI that he was finding it difficult to make ends meet.

The eldest Carbonell son, Hector, was fired from his job at the post office because the government claimed he was Communist. And George was kicked off his West Tampa All-Star Baseball Team just prior to the team leaving to compete in the national all star tournament in California for wearing a "26th of July" hat to practice. "I was on the same team as Lou Piniella," said George. "We won our region and we were real good. I was just a kid, maybe 12. It was heartbreaking."

George said the most humiliating moment for the family was the night someone threw an open bucket of red paint at their home. The guilty party did so while driving by, missed their home and hit their neighbor's car. "My mother ran outside with a rag and tried all night to clean the car," remembered George. "She apologized to the neighbor for a week straight. She was so embarrassed and felt awful."

The situation only grew worse over the next few months as the isolation of Cuba became U.S. policy. On October 19, 1960, the U.S. imposed a trade embargo against Cuba; Cuba responded on October 25 by nationalizing all U.S. properties left on the island. The result was that on January 3, 1961, the U.S. officially broke off diplomatic relations with Cuba, and finally, on January 14, 1961, the 26th of July Movement was officially dissolved in Tampa.

"In a meeting that took place a few days ago, we decided to close the '26th of July Club', not for the depredations of some individuals that call themselves anti-communists in order to carry out criminal acts in Tampa, but because the government of the United States has broken off its relations with Cuba," wrote Victoriano Manteiga in the January 13, 1961 edition of *La Gaceta*.

Carlos, though, refused to back down from his pro-Castro stand. When the FBI questioned him in front of his home in October 1961, the notes filed in his report stated that "he did not think that the present government in Cuba was communistic, although he stated that to him the present government in Cuba was doing the same thing in Cuba which Henry Ford had done when he started to build automobiles in Michigan. That is Ford put up the money and told the workers that if they would work they could share the profits of the business and the same thing is true in Cuba with the government putting up the money for various projects in Cuba and the poor people who never had anything under Batista were finding a better way of life. Possibly this was socialism but he could not see where it could be called communism. Cuban ties with Russia were out of economic necessity."

Carlos vocalized this opinion throughout Tampa, and the harassment continued.

The Carbonells could not take the persecution any longer. Following Castro's victory, Carlos was promised a job in Cuba if he ever wanted to return to his native country. In December 1960, he took the Cuban government up on their offer. Miami still had direct flights to Cuba, but he was afraid if he openly tried to leave the United States, the FBI would detain him and perhaps not allow him to leave. So Carlos Carbonell flew to New York and drove into Canada, where he then boarded a transport plane that was carrying eggs to Cuba. Upon arrival, the government lived up to its promise and gave him a job as a pressman for *La Bohemia*.

A few months later, George, his brother and his mother decided to join Carlos in Cuba. Rather than sneaking out of the country, they decided to go to Cuba via Miami. Perhaps they should have snuck out, as Immigration told George that because he was leaving the U.S. for Cuba, they were permanently taking away his U.S. residency and he would never be allowed to return, even to visit family.

"I wasn't a U.S. citizen," he explained. "My mother was born and raised in Tampa and my father was a citizen through marriage, but I was born in Cuba and never became a citizen. I was allowed to stay in the U.S. through a residency card. But they told me if I went to Cuba they would renounce my residency and never allow me back. I figured I'd be in Cuba for the rest of my life so I didn't care."

When they arrived in Cuba, they were reunited with Carlos, who was living in the Buzon Hotel in a beach community outside of Havana while waiting for the government to issue him the home he was promised. They quickly learned that life in Cuba would not be much easier than it was in the U.S.

The entire country was under emotional duress, explained George, as counter-revolutionary activities were the norm. George said 75 percent of Cuba was pro-Castro, but members of the other 25 percent would set off bombs in buildings. Anti-Castro Cuban-Americans would also launch missions from Miami, sailing boats near the Cuban shores and firing machine guns into the cities. On one occasion, George said that a 50-caliber machine gun rattled a home so badly that pieces of the ceiling fell into a baby's crib. Luckily, the baby was not injured, but such incidents kept the island nation on edge and on alert at all times.

George, though, tried to make the best of the tense situation. "I was only 16, so I was always out trying to have fun," explained George, "which often got me into trouble."

For instance, he and his friends threw a smoke bomb into a movie theatre as a practical joke, not realizing the implications of what they were doing. The armed guards in that neighborhood mistook it for an act of sabotage by anti-Castro forces, chased the boys down and arrested them. When the police realized it was just a case of boys being boys, they were released, but not before being cautioned to temper their rambunctious ways. George did not listen.

A short while later, he and his friends were again horsing around, this time at night, running through the streets. George turned a corner on a full sprint and almost ran into an armed guard, who out of instinct cocked his machine gun and took aim. Luckily for George, the guard realized it was just a teen playing around and not a counterattack.

A month or two after the Carbonells joined their patriarch in Cuba, the family moved to a condo on the beach. They had a beautiful home and Carlos had a good career. Life should have been getting better; instead, it only got worse. On December 2, 1961, Castro officially announced that Cuba was adopting the Communist form of government.

"My father always believed that Castro was pushed into Communism by the U.S. government," said Carbonell. "That doesn't mean he agreed with Communism. No, my father did not like Communism and it put him in a tough spot. My father left for Cuba expecting to live similarly as he did in the United States. He expected to be able to live where he wanted to live, shop where he wanted to shop, and eat what he wanted to eat. But then Cuba turned Communist and that all changed. The government controlled everything. At that point, a lot of people wanted to get out, my family included."

George said he regularly met groups of men and women planning to escape Cuba via boat and on more than one occasion he was offered a spot. He refused because he did not want to leave his parents behind and because he knew if they were caught they would be either jailed or executed.

Come October 1962, George began to wish he had taken the opportunity to flee. "The Cuban Missile Crisis arrived," he said. George said that the Cuban people were sure that the United States would attack, so they mobilized the entire country. Every adult male was provided a gun and given a section of Cuba to protect. Carlos, who was still at La Bohemia, was told to protect the area around the newspaper's offices.

"All the beaches were filled with anti-aircraft stuff and men with machine guns," he said. "I remember hearing someone firing into the air and a friend and me ducked and ran. It was a scary moment. I don't know what they were shooting at, but at that moment I thought the attack had begun.

"Then around 3 a.m. one day our home was rumbling with the sound of tanks being brought through a tunneled road leading to the beach. I knew a guy who was a bus driver and he told me to come with him to take a trip to see what was going on. People were everywhere with backpacks and military uniforms, mobilizing. It was tense."

Of course, the crisis passed and cooler heads prevailed. The Russians agreed to remove the missiles and the U.S. called off their warships.

"The Cuban people felt betrayed by the Russians," said George, continuing, "The Cubans were angry [at the Americans]." He explained that a common sentiment was that the U.S. government supported Batista, a tyrant, for years, so how dare they tell the Cuban people who should be their leader.

"The Cubans were ready to fight," clarified George. U.S. historians have long believed the Cubans would have supported the U.S. invasion. "If the invasion would have come, they would not have laid down their weapons or supported the U.S. They were ready to defend their country."

Following the Cuban Missile Crisis, the Carbonells decided enough was enough. Not only did they not agree with Communism, but the threat of war was too great. This was not the type of country in which they wanted to live.

They were returning to the United States. His mother did not want to do it on a rinky-dink boat under the veil of darkness, though. That was too risky. Instead, they asked the Cuban government for permission to return to the United States. George, his brother and his mother were granted the opportunity. Carlos was not. It would have been an embarrassment to the Cuban government for a revolutionary and employee of its official newspaper to leave the country.

In late 1962, a day before George and his mother were scheduled to leave Cuba, the G2–Cuba's political police–came to the Carbonells' home and took inventory of what they owned. They were told what they could take with them to the United States–a few pairs of clothes–and they confiscated the rest of their belongings, including George's gold chain and his mother's jewelry.

The next day, they boarded a plane and an hour later they landed in Miami. Despite the threats to never allow him back in the country, George was indeed welcomed back, but not before being questioned three hours a day for two days by the FBI on everything he had seen in Cuba. When the FBI realized he did not have any important military information to share, they allowed him, his brother and his mother to return to Tampa to start their lives over.

Six months later, George enlisted in the military for a two-year term. During his time in the military–the exact month and year escapes George–his father escaped from Cuba and returned to the U.S. He said his father had friends in the Cuban secret police who felt bad for him; he was separated from his family and not allowed to ever see them again. Carlos' friends knew of a flight leaving for Mexico late one night and told Carlos to be at the terminal. His friends then led him onto the plane, using their credentials to convince the airline that Carlos was to be given a seat because he had important "press business" to tend to in Mexico. When Carlos arrived in Mexico, he went right to the U.S. Embassy, asked for asylum and was allowed to return to Tampa.

George said that his father was questioned off and on by the FBI over the next few years, but the Cubans who once bullied the family left them alone.

Over the next few decades, according to George, Carlos rarely spoke of the Cuban Revolution or his work with the "26th of July Movement." In 1992, Carlos passed away. His obituary only listed him as a cigar maker and a native of Cuba.

George said his father was always a quiet man, never the type to wear his emotions on his sleeve, but he believes his father remained a tortured soul for the remainder of his life. While his father vehemently stated that he had no regrets supporting Castro during the Cuban Revolution, George said his father must have been bothered by the direction Cuba took. George said that his father did not work to turn Cuba into a Communist nation. He only wanted it to be free.

"At the end of the day, all my father ever wanted was a free Cuba," said George. "That's it. And he never got it."

As the calendar pages turned and the 1960s became the 70s, a new type of man stole the spotlight and front page headlines. In the early 1900s, wild men terrorized the night. In the mid-1900s, gangsters and Revolutionaries hid in the shadows. And in the late 1900s and early 2000s, Tampa became known as a sex capital. The man who bridged the gap from mafia to sex capital was Bobby Rodriguez, a man who dipped his hands in both worlds.

Chapter 9
Tampa's Man in Black

Originally published in *La Gaceta* newspaper on June 29, 2007

Author's Note: Bobby Rodriguez passed away in 2011. As far as I know, this was the one and only time he helped a journalist with such a lengthy exposé on his life. He was always such a private man. I decided to keep the article written as is for this book – as though he was still alive, which he was when it was originally published – because I believe it captures him better in its original form than if I was to rewrite it as a postmortem story.

Coolly hiding in the Palmetto bushes next to the Tanga Lounge on the Courtney Campbell Causeway, his hands wrapped tightly around his riot shotgun. He was waiting for them to come.

Them...The day before, Bobby Rodriguez, owner of the Tanga Lounge, refused a handful of bikers patronage to his strip club. These bikers had a reputation for breaking up bars. Rodriguez heard it started with a handful of the gang visiting a bar. Slowly, week by week, more and more became regular patrons until they had an army present. Once they established their dominant presence, they'd ruin the bar. They'd verbally abuse customers, steal money from the dancers, and turns some of the dancers into their own personal prostitutes. Rodriguez wasn't just another bar owner, though. He'd dealt with men like this before. And he'd deal with this biker gang in the same manner, the only manner in which men like this understand.

The previous day, he surrounded the bikers with his security team and tossed them from the bar, telling them to never come back. As the bikers obliged, they warned Rodriguez that they'd be back with more men. An arrogant Rodriguez replied, "Just make sure you can all handle the cover charge."

As a soft rumbling could be heard in the distance, Rodriguez checked his shotgun to make sure he had the cover charge they'd need to handle. Yep, it was loaded.

The rumble grew louder and more violent. Birds hiding alongside Rodriguez launched into the air, flying as far away from this pending war zone as possible.

Led by a white van, the motorcycle gang pulled into the parking lot next door to the Tanga Lounge. Rodriguez knew what was inside that white van – a cache of weapons. If they got to the van, the Tanga Lounge would be theirs. As the bikers dismounted and the rumble of their bikes went silent, the echoing of the cock of a shotgun froze them in their tracks. From his hiding spot, Rodriguez warned them, "Get back on your fucking bikes and leave or I will blow all your bikes up right now!" One of the bikers took a step forward, testing Rodriguez. In the dead silence that permeated the area, the bikers could hear one of Rodriguez' rings tapping the trigger of the riot shotgun. The bikers couldn't see him, but they could feel Rodriguez' presence. They knew he couldn't shoot all of them, but he'd at least shoot a few of them before they found him. While these bikers had a reputation for breaking up bars, Rodriguez had a reputation for placing bullets where they counted if you pressed him. Were any of them willing to chance that they'd be one of the men who didn't take a bullet?

"Get the fuck away from my bar right now!" screamed Rodriguez, not a quiver in his voice. He screamed it sternly, reminding the bikers that he did not toss around idle threats.

With that, the bikers back peddled, climbed on their bikes and sped down the Courtney Campbell Causeway in search of a different and easier bar to break up.

Today, despite time wilting away his once powerful body, the 71-year-old retired Tampa strip club pioneer hasn't lost that 1970s-style bad ass bravado that enabled him to introduce first GoGo bars and later full nude bars to Tampa, and allowed him to stay atop Tampa's adult entertainment industry for so many years. With slicked back hair, he struts around his waterside home hidden among the trees of Sulphur Springs, leaning his body on his clear glass cane whenever he feels the need. He may be aging and he may need a little assistance, but he still has style and a reputation to uphold.

He proudly shows off his back office to anyone who visits his home. It's a shrine to the type of man he is. The wall outside for the front door of the office showcases a shooting range target full of well-placed shots along the head and chest.

"I've never shot at a man further than 15 feet from me," boasted Rodriguez, who has been legally carrying a gun since the 1960s when he was then-Senator Tom Whittaker's personal bodyguard and drinking buddy. "If they are further than 15 feet and they don't have a gun, then they ain't a threat to you."

Inside the office, the walls are adorned with photos of true Tampa icons standing side-by-side with Rodriguez – governors, senators and political king makers. Many of the photos are of the late-publisher of *La Gaceta* newspaper, Roland Manteiga. To this day, Rodriguez can't speak of his late-friend without breaking down into tears.

"I loved him so much," admitted Rodriguez, who may have made a living on the fringe of the law, but always has been a nice guy at heart. That might be why so many of his good friends are community leaders.

"For some reason people think I'm a gangster," laughed Rodriguez, pointing to the many Ferdie Pacheco paintings hanging around his house. Pacheco, another of his best friends, has given six original paintings to Rodriguez, each one of gangsters or half naked women. "I have honestly only been arrested once in my entire life. My bars were always legal. I never got involved in any illegal activity. No one ever gambled in my bars and my girls only danced, they were never prostitutes. I made too much money legally to risk losing my bars due to illegal activities."

Taking a sip of his Heineken, Rodriguez inspected his knuckles, or rather the part of his hand where knuckles should be present. Years of fights have crushed his knuckles, rendering the back of his hand almost smooth.

"No, I'm no gangster, but if a man crossed me I'd kick his ass," boasted Rodriguez, who never talks, but rather screams every word. Even when he whispers he does so in a screaming whisper, spit flying from his mouth as often as curse words. His brash, ballsy, tough guy voice and lingo provide the perfect tone for his stories of being a one-time prince of Tampa's nightlife who stood side-by-side with some of its most notorious individuals – Pat Matassini, Jimmy Donofrio, Frank Diecidue and the Trafficantes.

"I may have never broken the law, but I had no problem pushing the boundaries of the law," laughed Rodriguez.

And it was this pushing that helped usher in the age of Tampa's adult entertainment through the famous (or infamous, depending on whom you are) bars he owned – The Deep South Lounge, Tampa's first GoGo bar and a rough country bar that was as likely to serve up a fight as it was a drink; The Godfather Lounge, a mafia-styled GoGo bar that briefly earned the ire of the Trafficantes because they thought the bar's name and décor was a dig on their family (it was actually designed and named for *The Godfather* movie); the Dream Bar, a popular watering hole among Tampa's organized crime members in the 1950s and 60s before Rodriguez took it over and turned it into an "everyman" type of bar; and the Tanga Lounge, one of the granddaddies of Tampa's full nude bars.

He's a businessman second and a father first, though. Not wanting to be the face of strip clubs, fearing it would have a negative impact on his children when they were young kids, he was the silent partner of many of his establishments, allowing his other partners to enjoy the fame and fortune that came with being a Tampa outlaw.

"And the police harassment," clarified Rodriguez. "If you wanted to be the face of a full nude bar, you'd get a lot of attention from men and especially women, but also a lot of attention from the police, who would continue to arrest you just to arrest you, never with a real reason. I didn't want that life. Some men enjoy the attention. Not me."

Bobby Rodriguez' importance in the annals of Tampa's history cannot be denied, but because he spent his career as the man behind the curtain, little is known about this pioneer of Tampa nude clubs. If the name Bobby Rodriguez is mentioned to the average Joe on the street, most will ask, "Who is Bobby Rodriguez?"

So who is Bobby Rodriguez? He's a true Tampa legend and relative unknown. He's famous and infamous. He's a bully and a hero. He's the man in black and the man in white. He's a protective father of daughters and the former boss of young women who stripped for money. He's living breathing irony.

But in the beginning, he was just a simple boy from West Tampa.

Las Vegas – the kingdom of nightlife. Sitting at a casino bar, not the lights of the strip, the blinging of the slot machines, nor the roar of the winners and whines of the losers at the table games could distract Rodriguez. All he could focus on were those legs. They were perfect, thought Rodriguez, long, sleek and with the right amount of muscle tone. The dress the owner of the legs wore was cut all the way to her butt, enabling Rodriguez to study every last inch of them. Finally, legs' owner rose from her chair and sashayed into the casino. Rodriguez wiped a drop of drool from his chin and frantically turned to his friend, "Did you see that broad sitting next to me? Did you see her legs?"

His friend stared incredulously at him for a few moments, waiting for Rodriguez to finish his thought, but that was all Rodriguez had to say.

"You stupid son of a bitch," said his friend. "That was Betty Grable!"

Rodriguez looked in the direction the woman had walked. There she was, Betty Grable, now at a table with Harry James, the Dorsey Brothers and a group of four or five other musicians.

"I never made it past her legs to look at her face," gushed Rodriguez to his friend before breaking up into laughter.

At that point, though, Rodriguez knew the nightclub business was for him. He decided when he returned to Tampa, somehow, someway, he'd open his own bar. And he knew he'd be successful. After all, he ran a successful business when he was just a little boy.

Born in West Tampa on August 5, 1935, his father, Fernando, was a cigar roller at Corral Wodiska and later an electrician. His mother, Amelia, was a homemaker. Money was always tight in the household and Rodriguez sought to contribute in any way he could. When he turned 8 years old, Rodriguez put away the .22 single shot rifle he hunted swamp rabbits with along the Hillsborough River, deciding fun time was over, and went to work.

These were the Wild West days of Tampa history with Charlie Wall, bolita games and shootouts in broad daylight. There were plenty of easy ways to make money. Some of his friends ran bolita numbers, but Rodriguez chose the high road. He purchased a shoe shining kit and set up camp outside the West Tampa Centro Español. Within weeks he built a steady clientele and claimed that corner as his own. Other boys would shine shoes on the corner on occasion and Rodriguez was fine with them, as long as they understood who owned that corner. When a large Italian boy showed up one day thinking his size and ethnicity would intimidate Rodriguez away from that prosperous corner, Rodriguez took him into an alley and told him otherwise.

"I beat him bad, so bad I never saw him in town again," remembered Rodriguez.

By the time he was 10 years old, Rodriguez saved enough money to buy his mom her first washing machine.

"One of the best moments of my life," he said. "I enjoyed earning my own money and helping my family."

He enjoyed it so much that at 13 years old he dropped out of Jefferson High School and moved to Key West in search of fulltime employment. While working at a tire shop just a few weeks after arriving in Key West, a juvenile officer stopped by the shop for a tire repair. Upon meeting Rodriguez he immediately asked his age, to which Rodriguez honestly responded. A few days later, a truant officer visited Rodriguez at the tire shop and sent him to school.

His return to school didn't last long, though. Less than one year later, still in Key West, Rodriguez dropped out again and worked first at a cola factory and later as a roofer. When he turned 18 he enlisted in the Air Force and was stationed in California working for Strategic Air Command as an electrician. Shortly after returning from his fateful trip in Las Vegas, he took a job as manager of a USO club near his Air Force base and began to learn the trade of bar management. When he finally returned to Tampa in 1956 he was ready to earn his fortune.

As a drunken Bobby Rodriguez stumbled around his house and looked out the window, he couldn't get over how many police cars were in his driveway. But he wasn't worried. The police cars weren't there to arrest him for his drunkenness; they were at his house drinking with him, as was a Florida senator.

One of the officers stumbled to the door, murmuring he was going to drive home. When he attempted to shift his police car into drive, in a drunken haze he accidentally shifted the car in reverse and drove it into a ditch. The car was totaled, but the officer was ok, so Rodriguez brought him back inside and promised they'd get the car out in the morning.

Later in the evening, Rodriguez' house lit up with a window reflection of a police siren flashing in his yard. A young officer had driven by the house and spotted the police car in the ditch. Confused as to what was going on and why so many police cars were parked in this neighborhood, he began writing down all the license plate numbers to report to his superior. Rodriguez tried to coax the highest ranked officer present to go outside and talk to the man, but he refused. After he had written down the license plate numbers, the officer pounded on Rodriguez' front door demanding answers. Finally, the chief answered the door and spoke to the officer. A few minutes later the officer left.

"The chief promoted the man," laughed Rodriguez. "It was a wild night." Pretty much every night had been wild for the past few months, though.

Upon returning from California, Rodriguez took a few odd jobs around town as an electrician while looking for employment in the bar business. He'd heard a good place to network with local business professionals was at a Hillsborough County Young Democratic Club, so off he went. At the first meeting he met State Representative Tom Whitaker, who was running for U.S. Senate. Not only did Rodriguez vow to support Whitaker's campaign, but the two became drinking buddies. When Whitaker became Senator Whitaker, he hired Rodriguez as his personal bodyguard and the two men spent night after night together, traveling from bar to bar.

"He was a real wild man," remembered Rodriguez. "He was a big man and when he started drinking he'd get out of hand. I wasn't his bodyguard to protect him from other people. I was his bodyguard to protect him from himself."

It was through Whitaker that Rodriguez became friends with law enforcement officers, and later Jimmy Donafrio, that man who would give Rodriguez his first job in the Tampa bar industry.

Besides being a well-known gambler, loan shark and Trafficante associate, Donafrio also owned a string of liquor stores, Rio Liquor Stores, throughout Tampa Bay. Managing all five or six of the stores, Rodriguez quickly made a name for himself not only as a hard worker, but an honest man. Rodriguez said Donafrio, who was used to dealing with petty thieves who would steal candy from a baby, was impressed that his registers were never short a dollar under Rodriguez' watch. In return for Rodriguez' loyalty, Donafrio paid him well and taught him everything there was to know about owning a bar.

By the mid-1960s Rodriguez was ready to set out on his own. With a $10,000 loan from his father, which Rodriguez paid back within the year, he purchased The Deep South Lounge, a popular but rough country bar located at 1705 W. Hillsborough Ave. that often welcomed nationally-known country singers one night and a wild bar fight and shoot out the next. Knowing Rodriguez would run a successful business, Donafrio also invested in the Deep South, and Rodriguez set out to turn the bar from a madhouse that was hemorrhaging money into a madhouse that made money. To do so, Rodriguez quickly set the precedent that the Deep South had room for only one troublemaker – him.

"I remember on one particular occasion this real tough guy came into the bar looking for a friend of mine named Tommy Wilson, saying he was going to kill him," said Rodriguez. "He walked right up to Tommy and pulled a gun. Well, he wasn't paying attention to me, so I snuck behind him, put my gun to his temple, grabbed his gun and slid it to my bartender. I then put my gun away and explained to the man that in my bar we don't handle our problems with guns. Before he could throw a punch, I hit him as hard as I could and then threw him right out the door into the street. When he landed, Tommy Wilson looked at the man and said to me, 'I've heard about it but I ain't never seen it. He's peeing his pants!' Yep, I knocked the piss out of him."

On another occasion, a young Italian man nicknamed Sampson for his tremendous strength had too much to drink and began slapping around an old man at the Deep South. Rodriguez and his staff struggled, but threw the strong man out. A few weeks later Rodriguez arrived at work to find his kitchen on fire. The fire department extinguished the flames before they spread to the rest of the bar and deemed the cause of the fire to be arson. A few hours later, Rodriguez received a call at the bar.

"The man asked me, 'How do you like that fire I set?' I recognized the man's voice right away," said Rodriguez. "It was Sampson. I didn't say a thing, though. I instead let him believe I didn't know who it was."

When Rodriguez bumped into Sampson again, though, he made it very clear that he knew he'd set the fire.

"He set my kitchen on fire so I set his ass on fire," laughed Rodriguez. "A Colt .45 automatic did the trick. I put a hole right in his fucking leg. He wanted to press charges, but he was a small time crook who sold his goods out of a bar located on a piece of property owned by a few of my friends. These friends used to come to the Deep South because they loved our barbeque, so they told Sampson if he testified against me or ever tried to hurt me he'd never be allowed to sell his goods on their property again. After that, he had a complete loss of memory."

Sampson had actually done Rodriguez a favor by torching the kitchen. Despite the business the Deep South's barbeque brought the establishment, Rodriguez said the kitchen staff would rip him off whenever they could, heisting giant bags of shrimp. Tired of searching for trustworthy employees and tired of being robbed, Rodriguez closed the kitchen less than a year after purchasing the Deep South.

Perhaps Rodriguez' highest hurdle in cleaning up the Deep South's image, though, was himself. Still good friends with Senator Whitaker and Tampa's law enforcement, the party moved from Rodriguez' house to his bar. On occasion,

Rodriguez would ask the band to continue to perform long after the bar had closed so the senator and law enforcement officers could continue to party. On these occasions, the night would usually end with everyone pulling their guns and shooting empty bottles.

"In the morning I'd have a headache and a real mess to clean up and curse myself," smiled Rodriguez.

About a year after opening the Deep South Lounge, Rodriguez tired of working with Donafrio. It was nothing personal; they had different views on how to run the business and began to butt heads on a regular basis.

Rodriguez had grown close with another local bar owner, Pat Mattasini, a mob-connected former cop. Mattasini agreed to buy Donafrio's share of the Deep South to unburden Rodriguez of his unpleasant business partner. Despite Mattasini's shady past, Rodriguez was not worried he would bring unlawful activities to the Deep South.

"Pat Matassini respected my wishes," said Rodriguez. "One time someone brought some counterfeit 20s into the Deep South and I threw them right out. I said, 'Get off my property," showed them my gun and they never came back. When Pat heard about it he didn't say a word. He understood how I felt about that stuff."

The Deep South's nighttime business was flourishing. With the nationally known country bands frequenting the establishment, it was rare to visit the bar on a weekend night and see it anything but packed from wall to wall. The daytime business, though, was suffering and eating up their profits. At the time, the Tampa International Airport was under construction, so there were plenty of working men in the area they could lure to the bar for mid-afternoon drinks, but they needed a hook.

"Men like women we thought," remembered Rodriguez. "Men will come to a bar with beautiful women. We were right."

A short time later, Rodriguez and Mattasini made the Deep South Tampa's first GoGo bar.

Some have claimed that the idea behind the GoGo bar came to Rodriguez when watching one of his premiere female singers perform. She was talented, one of the most talented singers to ever grace a stage in the Tampa Bay area, but she was also one of the most buxom women to ever grace a stage in the Tampa Bay area. Men packed the place to see her. Rodriguez thought, "I bet I can just toss a half-naked woman on stage and these same men would come every night." The singer who inspired him, according to some Tampa old-timers, was Dolly Parton. Rodriguez never made this claim, but countless old-timers have.

At first the dancers wore bathing suits, but as time went on and more and more men flocked to the bar – afternoon and night – to see these scantily clad women, the outfits became skimpier and skimpier until they were down to thongs and pasties. The bar was under constant scrutiny by the police. They would make regular visits and if one pubic hair was showing or any part of a nipple was exposed, they'd hand out citations. The constant police hassle only helped Deep South's legend grow. They were fighting against "The Man," pushing the boundaries of social acceptance. And with that, a new era in the history of Tampa's adult entertainment began with Bobby Rodriguez and Pat Matassini as the forefathers. Soon, though, a third person would join their ranks – Joe Redner.

"That old truck is an embarrassment to this bar," thought Rodriguez of the young Joe Redner's truck. It blew black exhaust smoke into the parking lot whenever he came to work and sounded like it was ready to break down at any minute, rumbling down the road like it was a lawnmower. Worst of all, though, its looks fit its noise. It had chipped and peeling paint, dented side boards and it was missing the passenger door. What amazed Rodriguez most of all, though, was despite the crummy truck, Redner was still a stud with the women.

Rodriguez noticed Redner eying up the new Honda motorcycle he'd recently purchased. Redner was a good employee. Introduced to him in 1972 through Matassini, Rodriguez quickly took to the youngster as he reminded Rodriguez of himself. Most importantly, since Redner took over as manager, the register was never missing a penny. To reward him for his honesty, Rodriguez decided to give Redner the motorcycle.

With Redner running the Deep South, it allowed Rodriguez to open new bars. In 1974 he opened the Godfather Lounge, a decadent mafia-themed GoGo bar located on the corner of Hillsborough Avenue and Manhattan Avenue that honored Rodriguez' favorite movie, *The Godfather*. The walls were adorned with pictures from the film and a glass case on the front wall was filled with sawed off shotguns, Tommy guns and other legendary mafia tools.

"It was a popular bar," said Rodriguez. But, not everyone liked it.

Santo Trafficante's brother, Fano, and underboss Frank Diecidue visited Rodriguez one evening demanding to know what was going through his mind, stating that Santo Trafficante, Jr. was furious with Rodriguez for opening a bar openly mimicking organized crime. After Rodriguez explained that it was mimicking a movie, all was well, and not only were they all friends again, but Fano sold Rodriguez The Dream Bar, located at 2801 Nebraska Ave. Once known for being a hotspot among gangsters in the 1950s, Rodriguez turned it into a GoGo bar and made a profit on what was a dying business. Soon after, Rodriguez also purchased a bar in Haines City and a few bars in Key West.

In 1975, while driving home from the Deep South one evening, Redner heard on the radio news that the Supreme Court had ruled that full nudity was no longer considered obscene. Excited about the money a full nude bar could make, he pitched the idea to Rodriguez, who thought it could work but did not want to risk such a risqué proposition on one of his established GoGo bars. Instead, with Rodriguez' support, Redner opened the Night Gallery on Hillsborough Avenue. Police arrested Redner on a regular basis, always looking for ways to shut the bar down. But they always failed. Redner would be released soon after his arrest, no charges levied, and the Night Gallery continued to make money. Encouraged by the financial success of the Night Gallery, Rodriguez decided to open a full nude bar as well. With children to think about and not wanting their classmates to know their father ran a full nude bar, Rodriguez asked Redner to be his partner. Rodriguez would put up the money and Redner would be the face of the bar.

In 1977 the Tanga Lounge was born. Located near the Tampa International Airport along the Davis Causeway (now the Courtney Campbell Causeway), Rodriguez wanted the bar to have a tropical feel. He named it the Tonga Lounge after the Hawaiian god "Tonga." An employee filled out the paperwork with the city wrong, writing "Tanga" by accident. Rather than going through the hassle of correcting the name, Rodriguez stuck with the name Tanga, which he learned a short time later was actually the name of an obscure island in the South Pacific.

"It all worked out," said Rodriguez.

Though Night Gallery was first, Tanga Lounge became the more renowned of the two full nude clubs among law enforcement. The police would raid the club at least twice a day, arresting the management and dancers. Rodriguez said it got to the point in which they had a bus trekking back and forth between the Tanga Lounge and the police station, bailing out one group of employees, dropping them off at the Tanga Lounge, and then heading back to the police station to bail out the recently arrested employees. But, in time, the city decided to abide by the Supreme Court ruling that nudity was not obscene, paving the way for nude clubs to open up all over Tampa.

"They never arrested me," said Rodriguez. "Joe was the face of the Tanga and the one they were after. They'd walk right past me and arrest him. I used to send him to the law library so he could read up on law and learn how to keep himself out of jail and the Tanga out of trouble. I swear he read so much about law that he could pass the bar exam right now. Joe is a brilliant man."

Between Redner's knowledge of the law and Rodriguez' firm stance to keep criminals and shady practices out of the Tanga Lounge, the club rarely had any issues with the police once nude clubs were accepted as legal by the city. While some nude clubs opening up throughout the city allowed customers to disgrace the girls, Rodriguez would have none of that. Male employees, including management, were not allowed to date the dancers. The dancers could not date customers. Security guards walked every dancer to their car when they were off duty, preventing disorderly customers from hassling the girls. Dancers were only allowed to take breaks in groups of three and four, which prevented a dancer from secretly prostituting herself to customers on her break. If Rodriguez caught known criminals in the Tanga Lounge, he would forcefully remove them. If he learned of troublemakers coming to the club, such as the biker gang, he met the problem head on.

"Don't fuck around with my money," said Rodriguez. "And that's what troublemakers d o – they are messing with my money."

The Tanga Lounge became a Tampa landmark. Pilots used to make jokes that they knew they were in Tampa when they saw the Tanga Lounge's famous glowing peak from the s ky. (The peak was lost around 1997, though, when a homeless man accidentally set fire to a g arbage c an when he threw out a lit cigarette. The fire spread to the Tanga Lounge. It was extinguished, but not before it lost the famous peak.)

By t he m id-1980s, R odriguez a nd R edner's l ongtime f riendship a nd business relationship began to sour. Redner had opened other clubs on his own by then and said that Rodriguez was jealous. Rodriguez said he found Redner counting money at the club with one of the dancers by his side, which was in direct v iolation of h is rule – "Never a llow the d ancers n ear my money!" A fight erupted t hat s pilled o ut o nto t he c auseway. Rodriguez was arrested. Redner was choked unconscious and suffered two broken ribs.

Redner did not press charges and agreed to give up all managerial duties with the Tanga Lounge. He kept his partnership and was sent a share of the profits.

In 1986, t hree T ampa-area nightclubs that had been owned or operated by Redner caught fire. Authorities c harged Rodriguez with a rson b ut c harges were dismissed.

Rodriguez and Redner shared a volatile partnership t he next 20 years until December 3 1, 2 004 w hen the T anga Lounge was s hut down and soon after demolished to make way for the FDOT's Courtney Campbell Causeway widening project.

When the FDOT purchased the land, Rodriguez and Redner split a million dollars.

"What a good deal," said a sarcastic Rodriguez. "One year's salary."

For Rodriguez, it was an end of an era. The man who helped to usher in Tampa's GoGo e ra a nd later full-nude era was no longer part of the s cene. When the Tanga Lounge closed, Rodriguez spoke of reopening the club elsewhere, but a taste of retirement quickly changed his mind.

Rodriguez and Redner also made amends.

"I'm p roud o f J oe," s aid Rodriguez. "I a lways knew h ow s mart h e was.

Now that he's cleaned up his act I think people are stupid for not voting for him. He's been fighting the system for so long that he knows everything about it. He's one of the smartest men I've ever known and I know he'll be successful in everything he does."

While Redner's star continued to shine brightly, Rodriguez had no regrets about choosing the quiet life behind the curtain.

"All that matters is what my family thinks about me" said Rodriguez in his classic screaming tone. "I don't care what people think about me and who knows who I am. I never have. If people remember me, if no one remembers me, so what?"

Another Tampa icon of the 1970s and 80s thought much differently. Gene Holloway would do seemingly anything to remain in the public eye.

The Dark Side of Sunshine

Chapter 10
The Man Who Rose from the Dead

Gene Holloway is alive...and, for the second time in his colorful life, people are shocked to hear it.

...Yes, that Gene Holloway...The cowboy hat and boots wearing, sky diving, mountain climbing, woman-chasing, alcohol tasting, exotic animal owning and life of the party whose rags to riches story captivated Tampa Bay in the 1970s and 1980s. Yes, that Gene Holloway. The man who once owned the eighth most profitable restaurant in the nation–the Sea Wolf–married a former Miss Tampa, collected dozens upon dozens of priceless antiques just to brag about how much money he spent, ran for president and tried to bribe the pope to come to dine at his restaurant. Yes, that Gene Holloway. The man who at the height of his popularity and seemingly at the height of his riches was accused of torching his home and then "disappeared" in the Gulf of Mexico one night when he fell off his boat in 1981. Yes, that Gene Holloway–the man who was pronounced dead, only to be arrested for supposedly dealing drugs in Canada a few months later. Yes, that Gene Holloway. If you have never heard of Gene Holloway, everything printed above is 100 percent true. While it seems like the plot of a blockbuster summer movie, it is actually the true life story of a Tampa man.

Yes, that Gene Holloway is still alive. However, he barely resembles the Gene Holloway who once captivated Tampa Bay.

His famous trademark cowboy attire has been retired to a storage facility somewhere in Odessa. His Kenny Rogers-esqe salt and pepper beard is now all salt. The only antiques he collects are those he finds while out treasure hunting on the coastline–some old coins, a few meteorites and some random items like discarded bottles. His exotic animals are a thing of the past. He does not even own a goldfish. He no longer desires to be the center of attention. The man who once embodied the fast-living, extravagant, buy-everything-you-want, party hard lifestyle that defined the 1970s and 1980s wants to leave that person in the past. He can't even remember the last time he was invited to a party, and hordes of guests stomping upon his pearly white carpets is the type of scenario that haunts his dreams; he now makes everyone who steps foot in his home remove their shoes.

Yes, it is the same Gene Holloway who once owned the front page headlines of Tampa Bay's daily newspapers. Yet, he appears to be a totally different Gene Holloway.

"I have not really changed too much," argued Holloway in a subdued manner that does not fit the abrasive personality he once showcased. "People like to think I did all these bad things, but the truth is I have only been in trouble with the law one time in my life and it was not for doing anything that could hurt others. I will not say that I have always lived my life like an angel, but I have always been a good person who wants to do good things for people."

"My father is a classic case of temptation," said Holloway's son, Randy. "We all like to think that we will act purely when temptation is thrown our way. The truth is most of us would not be able to resist from the start. My father came from nothing and became a self-made millionaire while still in his mid-30s. Then the temptation came. Everyone suddenly wanted to be his friend. Everyone had their hands out and everyone was handing him something. It was tough temptation to resist and he will admit to that. I think his story is one that people could learn from."

It is a story that begins on May 1, 1937 in Sulphur Springs, the date and place of his birth.

Gene Holloway Growing Up

His family was poor. Real poor. So poor that even as a toddler, an age in which children should see the world through rose-colored lenses, Holloway knew they were poor. Holloway's early life was spent living in a small shack along Route 41 near the phosphate pit at which his father worked. There were four siblings in all, Holloway being the second oldest. His sister was the oldest and he had two younger brothers, and they were the only four children they knew who did not own a single pair of shoes.

Life was far from perfect for the Holloways and it got even more difficult in the 1940s when his father enlisted in the merchant marines to serve his country during World War II. With their sole provider gone, the Holloways moved in with their maternal grandmother. It only provided temporary stability. His mother was caught cheating on his father with a soldier home from war. His father filed for divorce from overseas. This was a patriotic time in America. The troops were fighting for our freedom against an enemy unlike the world had ever seen. Any man risking his life was considered a hero and turning your back on a hero while he was still off at war was looked down upon immensely. Not only did the judge grant Holloway's father a divorce, he also ordered Holloway's mother to leave the state of Florida and never return. She was banned from ever seeing her children again.

Their father was still at war, though, and their grandmother could not handle four rambunctious children on her own. His sister stayed with the grandmother while 7-year-old Holloway and his two younger brothers were sent to live in a small two-story children's home located on hundreds of acres of land across the street from Ballast Point Elementary School. The home was owned by a woman Holloway only remembers as "Mother Hancock." She lived there with her own children and another 20 who, like Holloway, were displaced because of the war. Bunks were stacked in two bedrooms into which the children crammed. And the land was home to hundreds of hogs and cows, animals which the children tended.

"My father paid for us to live there and she also made money off the work we did," said Holloway. "Smart woman I guess."

In the mornings, Holloway milked the cows and fed the pigs. By day, he attended school. And at night, Holloway's job was to rub Ponds cream on Mother Hancock's face as all the children listened to the radio. He was also the home's official rat hunter. He would set traps throughout the home and was paid 25 cents a rat.

"I had a different upbringing," laughed Holloway. "And at least I had shoes for a while."

He often got into trouble; usually boys-will-be-boys type trouble like playing with another child's chemistry set against his will or sneaking candy into his room. No matter how innocent the crime, the punishment was always the same—lashes with a riding crop.

This was Holloway's life for five years. Then, the war ended and his father returned home to save Holloway and his brothers from the children's home. His father found work on a dredging team. Unfortunately, he did not have a home. Holloway's sister continued to live with the grandmother while Holloway, his brothers, his father and his father's new wife lived on an old yellow school bus they used to follow the dredging work. The children continued to go to school, attending whichever one was closest to where they parked. At night they would roll out makeshift beds of towels onto the bus floor while his father and step-mother slept in a pull out bed in the back of the bus. And Holloway again became the child with no shoes.

"My dad was a heavy drinker by that time," said Holloway. "He was not a very responsible person. In a way, my father is responsible for the man I became. I looked at him and knew I never wanted to be like him. I wanted to be successful."

They lived on that bus for three years before his father finally settled the family down in a small home in Drew Park in Tampa. Holloway attended Oak Grove High School, but school was secondary to him. He wanted to make money. He sold newspapers on the corner before school and later delivered doughnuts in Sulphur Springs, making the long trek to work each morning via bicycle. Within a few months' time he became supervisor to all the delivery boys, a job that equaled higher pay and all the doughnuts he could eat.

He dropped out of school during his senior year, got married and fathered a son, Daniel. He was making decent money for a teenager, had a beautiful bride and a new baby. Yet, something was missing–adventure. He had lived his whole life in one small section of the world and knew there was a lot more to see. All he had ever known were the poor streets of Tampa Bay. He wanted to experience life. The Navy provided him with the adventure he sought. He enlisted at the age of 17 and bid goodbye to his new family.

"He never was father of the year," said an angry Daniel.

Holloway was stationed aboard a ship that travelled to such exotic destinations as New Zealand, Australia and Antarctica. In New Zealand, he fell in love with mountain climbing. Florida is flat, after all, so he had never seen a mountain in person prior to joining the Navy. To Holloway, they were the ultimate test of his manhood, thousands of miles of treacherous rock screaming out to the paltry humans upon whom they look down on, "You are small and insignificant! You cannot possibly conquer me!"

Holloway earned his mountain climbing stripes on the rocky hills of New Zealand, but he earned legendary status on Mt. Erebus, the southernmost active volcano on Earth and one of the highest mountains in Antarctica. Snow was as much of a mystery to Holloway as mountains. It was one of the most beautiful sights he had ever seen. He wanted to run out into the Antarctic like a little boy and frolic about. So, when his commanding officers asked for volunteers to learn to man the dog sleds, Holloway leapt at the opportunity. By the end of his first visit to Antarctica he mastered controlling nine-dog sled teams. One particular trip on the sled brought him to the foot of Mt. Erebus. He wanted to conquer it and he promised himself that if he ever returned to Antarctica he would.

His ship returned the following year and he began telling his shipmates of his desire. Word travelled back to his captain, who called him into his quarters one afternoon and asked him if he was serious. Of course he was, he told the captain, he knew if given the opportunity he could make it to the top. Not only did the captain give him permission to make the climb, he wanted to tag along.

A few days later a team consisting of Holloway, the captain, an AP reporter, and a Cal Tech University professor began making their way up the mountain via banana sled.

The journey was difficult, but Holloway was 20 years old and nothing but rippling muscle. He could make it. The others, however, were suspect, specifically the captain who, while in good shape, was over 50 years old.

At around 2,000 feet, Holloway overheard the captain telling the reporter that he wanted to turn back, that he wanted to call a helicopter to come pick them up. Holloway was having none of that. He rushed into the captain's tent, where the conversation was taking place, and said he refused to go home. He wanted to make it to the top. The captain agreed to allow Holloway to continue. The reporter and the captain took the helicopter back to the ship. The professor continued with Holloway.

At around 8,000 feet a storm hit–a total white out. They did not have a radio to call for help, so they hunkered down in their tents

Holloway pictured here on Mt. Erebus, the southernmost active volcano on Earth and the highest mountain in Antarctica.

and prayed for survival. In their minds, death was inevitable. Holloway does not know how, but they survived the night. In the morning, the storm cleared and they were able to continue their journey. They made it to the top and looked into the giant crater, basking in the warmth of the volcanic steam.

The following morning, they began their trek home. A few thousand feet down, a helicopter spotted them and picked them up. The pilot was shocked that

they made it to the top. He informed Holloway that just a few weeks earlier, the great Sir Edmund Hillary, famously known for being the first to climb Mount Everest, failed to conquer Mt. Erebus, turning back at the first sight of a white out.

"That will always be one of my greatest accomplishments," he said. But it is far from one of his most famous. When he returned to Tampa a few years later, the seeds of the legend of Gene Holloway were planted.

Gene Holloway Starts His Career

By the age of 23 years old, he was married with two children. The Navy did not provide him with a skill-set for any particular career, but it taught him how to use his drive and determination in an organized way. "The U.S. military breeds organization," said Holloway.

He worked various odd jobs for a few years, primarily earning a living as a junk collector. If he found a broken piece of machinery that nobody wanted, he would take it, fix it and sell it for a nice profit. He made decent money, but the money was secondary to the sales experience he earned.

He found steady work with Food Enterprises, a food brokerage company that supplied restaurants and stores with their goods. He was a skilled salesman and, several years after he was hired, he was the top earner in the company. When the owner was killed in a car accident, the company was up for grabs. Holloway approached a gentleman he knew had the money to buy the company and pitched him on being partners. Holloway told the moneyman that if he bought the company, he would run it. They would be 50/50 partners and the moneyman would get rich without ever having to do one minute of work. The potential partner laughed at Holloway, telling him he was going to buy the company for his son and that he did not need Holloway to make the venture successful.

Holloway did not pout or sulk. Instead, he started his own food brokerage company, Service Brokerage Company. Many of his old clients went with him. He then added a number of new companies and after his first year in business he was over $70,000 richer–a lot of money to earn in those days–especially for a man who once lived on a bus and could not afford a pair of shoes.

Over the next few years, he was divorced, remarried, divorced, remarried again and then divorced again. While his love life was chaotic, his business was not. It continued to surge upwards. In 1968, he received a major break. A new restaurant called Red Lobster was opened in Lakeland, Florida and Holloway became its food broker. Within a few years' time, the solo restaurant exploded into 175 locations and Holloway was the broker for all of them. His company was worth millions, which is what he got for it when he sold it to General Mills in the early 1970s. At the age of 36, Gene Holloway was a self-made millionaire.

The first major purchase he made with his newfound riches was a 9,000-square-foot home on Lake Hollingsworth in Lakeland. This was just the first of many major purchases.

Gene Holloway Marries Former Miss Tampa

He met wife #4 in 1974 while skydiving in Zephyrhills. Her name was Debbie Ponton and she was gorgeous, a former Miss Tampa in fact. They both had an affinity for adventure and fast living. She was the type of woman he once only dreamt of dating. Once he was a millionaire, it was possible to win the heart of such a woman.

They dated for a year and were married in 1975. Most newspaper and magazine accounts in the past claimed they were married in 1979, but Holloway said they are wrong. It was 1975.

The wedding was as colorful as their marriage later became. They were married on Lake Hollingsworth in front of 400-500 of their closest friends. As Debbie waited at the altar, a C-47, which is a WWII military transport plane, flew overhead, depositing 30 skydivers as it passed. They formed a ring overhead the ceremony, a beautiful symbol for that special day. Then, the plane passed over one more time, jettisoning Holloway and two of his closest friends, Jim Hooper and Jeff Serles, from 10,000 feet.

It was the first time Holloway made a leap outside of the jump-friendly confines of an airport and the highest jump he'd ever attempted. True to his up-to-that-point storybook rise from rags to riches, he landed the jump perfectly; right on X marks the spot.

The new couple was a match made in the 1970s fast-lifestyle heaven.

They continued to skydive at higher and higher altitudes. They held lavish parties at their home. They bought extravagant artifacts and antiques from around the world. They even collected exotic animals–tigers, cougars, peacocks, Clydesdale horses and more.

"The animals were Debbie's idea," said Holloway. "She wanted the big cats so I said sure. Of course, after we bought them I got into them too. I can't lie about that. I loved those cats."

And they dressed the part of Tampa's new wild couple. Debbie was always beautifully adorned in the latest fashions while Holloway strutted around town in cowboy boots, a cowboy hat and rich rancher attire. He saw himself as a modern day cowboy, a man above the law, so he figured he should look the part.

He would soon learn, however, that no one is above the law.

Gene Holloway Opens The Sea Wolf Restaurant

He was too young to retire. He was in his mid-30s, had all the money he needed, a beautiful wife and was the life of the party, yet he was bored. Holloway may have been riding in the fast lane, but that was all a façade. He needed to be earning a living to be happy.

He'd partnered with a handful of people on seafood restaurants located throughout the state, but none of that made him happy. He was a not a "go along for the ride" type of guy. He needed to be THE man in charge. He enjoyed the restaurant business because he was good at it; his black book full of seafood connections from his years as a broker meant he could find the best deals in town. He was tired of using his connections to help make other people rich, however. He was ready to venture out on his own.

Holloway knew that each Red Lobster was earning close to $1 million a year. He thought he could do better. He thought he could open a more successful restaurant chain than Red Lobster. Because of the low prices at which he could buy seafood, he could sell it at a much cheaper price than Red Lobster, stealing their business away. His plan was to start with two restaurants–one in Tampa across from Busch Gardens and one in Lakeland–and when they became self-sufficient he would expand his empire throughout the state and later the nation.

He called his restaurant chain The Sea Wolf, named after the famous Jack London book about a hunting expedition in the Bering Sea. He read the book while stationed in Antarctica and the underlying Darwinian theme of survival of the fittest spoke to him. Considering from where he came and what he had done to survive, it was a fitting name for the restaurant. The décor would be just as fitting; it told each visitor exactly who Gene Holloway was—a wild, exotic, free spending man living in the fast lane. The Lakeland location was popular, but the Tampa location was his marquee, a home for his wild antique collection. As his menu once read:

"From the palm-studded parking lots adorned with ornate five-globe street lights, replicas of the lights that Teddy Roosevelt and the Rough Riders rode under on their way to embark to Cuba, to the hand-painted, stained and polished beveled glass, the Sea Wolf, like many of the museum pieces it contains, is a true masterpiece.

"Many authentic Louis Comfort Tiffany glass paintings are featured throughout the Sea Wolf. Truly a master of his art, the beauty is unequaled in his draped and plated glass. Holloway owns the largest collection of Tiffany stained glass in the world.

"Personally supervising over 100,000 hours of carpentry work that went into crafting the Sea Wolf, Holloway demanded perfection from the skilled craftsmen who created by hand the lattice, brackets and moldings inside."

The restaurant also featured a Steinway piano and two 1,000-gallon aquariums. It had windows overlooking gardens full of peacocks, palm trees and tropical plants. And it had a stable of Clydesdales that took customers from the parking lot to the restaurant.

The Tampa Sea Wolf seated over 500 people, yet on weekends it was a scramble to find a seat. With its prime location across from Busch Gardens, exotic and extravagant décor, and its delicious and affordable food, it quickly became THE place to dine. In 1979, it was listed as the eighth highest grossing restaurant in the United States, pulling in over $5 million in revenue.

Of course, the secret to the restaurant's success was also Holloway himself. Many people dined at the restaurant as much for the chance encounter of meeting him as they did for the food and décor. Holloway said he was well aware that personal fame could propel the restaurant to grander heights, so he continued to seek out ways to make the headlines–national headlines.

Gene Holloway Runs for President

Sometime in 1979 or 1980, Holloway said, he heard murmurings that his employees were talking about unionizing. A professor at University of South Florida (USF) put them up to it. The professor thought it would make for an interesting social experiment– watching students form a union. A number of his students worked at the restaurant and he told them that the backbone of America's workforce was the unions. If the employees ever expected to be fairly compensated for their work, the professor told his students, they needed to join together as one. Together we stand, united we fall.

The union fell.

Twelve students made up the pro-union team. Sea Wolf had over 150 employees, though. In order to unionize, the students needed to convince the rest of the employees to vote yes. This was a tall order. Most of the employees loved working for Gene Holloway. He treated them well. They also feared him. He was so controlling that when he heard rumors of employees stealing food, he installed a permanent lie detector test in the restaurant that he used on any suspects. Holloway was not a man employees wanted to cross.

The 12 students' plan was to win over their fellow employees by showing them that the community supported them. The students planned a rally across the street from the restaurant and invited friends, colleagues and pro-union advocates. If they could garner enough attention and make unionizing the richest restaurant in Tampa a citywide issue, perhaps they could swing the other employees to their side.

Holloway, however, was tipped off to the effort and decided to steal their thunder. He organized a carnival in his parking lot on the same day as the rally. He brought a host of his exotic animals to the parking lot, carnival rides and a day's worth of live entertainment, including himself wrestling a bear. Those dining at the restaurant could not see the picketing employees across the street through the thick circus crowd and those driving by paid the picketers no mind. How could they notice people with signs when cougars were roaming about?

The rally never got the attention it needed and the restaurant employees voted against unionizing. Holloway won.

"It was a brilliant plan," said Tony Zapone, one of Holloway's closest friends at the time. "And it really sums up what made him so successful. He knew the secret to the restaurant's success was to continue to generate all the attention."

If the Sea Wolf was going to become a nationally-recognized restaurant, it needed national publicity. It needed national PR stunts.

"I ran for president," Holloway laughed.

His reasons were two-fold. The primary reason was publicity, he said, and the secondary reason was the escalating gas prices. Gas prices were rising too high and the success of his business depended upon people from throughout the state driving to his restaurant. Higher gas prices also impacted the cost of food delivery. If gas was too high, he explained, he would lose big time money. At the end of 1979, he said he predicted the gas crisis would cost him up to $2 million in 1980.

One night in early 1980, while slamming back some drinks with his buddies from the Tampa Rough Riders, he babbled on and on about the nation's need for a better president and how the lack of leadership in President Jimmy Carter's administration is what led the nation to the current gas problem. He drunkenly pounded his fist into a table as he spoke passionately about what makes a great leader–drive, determination, fearlessness and a vision that works–and how he had not seen a capable man run for president in a long time. When he was finished his lament and sought to catch his breath, a voice from the back of the room yelled out, "Why don't you run Gene?! You'd make a great president." The rest of the room roared in approval. It was decided. Gene Holloway was going to run.

"We did not really think he could win," said Zapone, who acted as Holloway's press secretary. "But we wanted to run it like a real campaign. We thought if we could get some real push behind it, perhaps we could influence some of the other candidates and get them to support some of the things we wanted to see done. A nd, more importantly, if the Gene Holloway for p resident c ampaign could get real n ational attention, it would turn h im into a national c elebrity a nd help the restaurant."

His p arty a ffiliation was "The Bull M oose Party" in h onor of Theodore Roosevelt, who ran under that party n ame when h e was d enied the Republican Party nomination in 1912. The campaign printed buttons and T-shirts and bumper stickers that it mailed around the nation. They purchased billboard space in Tampa. Holloway spoke throughout the state on why he was running. They planned a n ational radio and television commercial campaign and even released a platform. Holloway spent a total of $30,000 o ver a few months before he pulled the plug on his campaign. Despite their best efforts, it was not garnering the type of national attention they had hoped.

"Besides," said H olloway, "when [Ronald] Reagan announced he was going to run, I figured I wasn't needed anymore. He was a fine candidate."

This was not h is only failed PR s tunt in 1 980. That s ame y ear, h e a lso tried to lure the pope to his restaurant with a priceless painting, *Baptism of Lithuania*, b y renowned Polish a rtist W ojciech Gerson. The painting depicts the marriage of Queen Hedwig of Poland and the Prince of Lithuania, a marriage that resulted in the conversion of Lithuania to Christianity. Holloway purchased the painting at an auction in New York and put it on display in his restaurant. A local bishop told Holloway that Pope John Paul II was Polish and would probably love to own that important painting, so Holloway announced that if the pope dined at the Tampa S ea Wolf he would give the painting to him. Holloway offered the painting both as a kind gesture to the pope and as a PR stunt. If the pope actually dined at the Sea Wolf, the restaurant would garner worldwide publicity.

The pope never dined at the restaurant.

"It was worth a try," lamented Holloway. "Then the next thing I knew, it was 1982 and I woke up one morning to see a black man in the corner of the room curling h is hair and another man s leeping o n a cot next to me. I was in prison. I remember saying to myself that it was all a dream, that I was not really in prison. I told myself that I would wake up in a few minutes and be in my own bed and the whole nightmare would be over. W ell, I didn't wake up for another five years. It was real. I was in prison for real."

Gene Holloway Fakes His Death

The house was gone, burned to the ground. There were no witnesses, yet investigators did not need long to finger their top culprit–the owner of the Thonotosassa h ome, G ene H olloway. T he timing was t oo p erfect, t hought investigators.

In 1981, Debbie Ponton filed for divorce, claiming she walked in on Holloway and his secretary having sex in the Thonotosassa home. In the divorce case, s he asked for the Thonotosassa h ome. The case was a long way from seeing a c ourt room, b ut Debbie already had a minor victory–a j udge granted h er an injunction barring Holloway from the home.

He agreed to stay away, but asked Debbie if he could throw one last party there. Debbie figured, "Why not?" so she and her brother, who was living with her at the house, stayed elsewhere on the night of April 14, 1981.

It was a particularly wild party and Holloway was particularly drunk, witnesses said. Witnesses also said that he was parading around the home, chest puffed out, bragging that he was going to burn the home so that his soon-to-be ex-wife received nothing. Witnesses c laimed he s aid on that evening that he was going to liquidate everything that she could take and then spend the money before the divorce was settled. He did not want to give her a penny of his money.

Witnesses also stated he s aid h e was g oing to u se the fire as another publicity stunt. They said he was bragging that he would light the house on fire, climb to the roof and parachute off, later boasting to the press that the fire was an attempt on his life by certain individuals who wished him dead.

"Yeah, a lot of people think I burned that house," said Holloway. "But I was not there when it started. I was real drunk that night, too drunk to drive, so a few of my friends picked me up and drove me [to my Lakeland home]. Somehow, that building blew up that night. Not sure how."

Investigators at the time were positive that Holloway did it and vowed to bring him to justice for arson.

This was just one of many problems Holloway was facing at the time.

According to investigators, he was in debt up to $4 million. He was earning good money off the restaurants but he was spending more.

In 1980, he sold his Lakeland restaurant for, according to Zapone, $250,000. Zapone said he made the deal for Holloway and then helped his friend secure a $210,000 loan from Second National Bank using stock as collateral. He then began putting out feelers for the Tampa restaurant. Zapone said he was negotiating with Busch Gardens to sell it for $2.5 million.

In addition, an anonymous source said that Holloway's life was in danger. The source said that Holloway's good friend Jeff Serles had been sentenced to up to 20 years in prison and asked Holloway to hide $750,000 for him. The source explained that Holloway thought he could spend the money on the restaurant and have plenty of time to earn it back, but Serles was released after only two or three years and was angry when he learned that Holloway did not have his money.

"Serles was the type of guy who would just as soon kill you as look at you," said the anonymous source. "Gene was scared."

Holloway admitted that his life was in danger, but he fingered a different culprit–Debbie Ponton.

He said that during happier marital times he took out a $10 million insurance policy on his life that he put in her name rather than his for tax reasons, which meant only she could cancel it. He made the payments each month, but after she filed for divorce he said he stopped making payments on the policy; it was the only way he could get it cancelled. He said that Debbie found out and she and her brother resumed the payments. Holloway said that soon after the payments were taken over someone put out a hit on his life with Jimmy Donofrio, a well-connected and feared man. He does not know if Debbie was behind the scheme, but he believes the hit had to do with the insurance policy.

Holloway has been telling this story for years. Both his sons echo this tale, as does the transcription of an interview he did with the University of South Florida's Special Collections Department in 2002.

He was in debt, there were threats on his life and he had a pending divorce case that he knew was going to be costly. He was ready to disappear.

In the summer of 1981, Holloway took out a new $16 million life insurance policy, this one listing one of his ex-wives as the beneficiary. Then, in a lease-purchase agreement, he handed over ownership of Tampa's Sea Wolf to Robert Dourney. Zapone said he sold it for $150,000 down and payments over the years that would total $750,000.

"Busch Gardens would not budge on the deal we wanted," explained Zapone. "I think we could have gotten more money, but Gene wanted to take this deal. Looking back, it is obvious why he was in a hurry to sell."

The deal was finalized on September 2, 1981, a day in which Holloway was on a week-long pleasure cruise in the Keys with a group of friends.

On September 4, 1981, the other passengers aboard the 44-foot trawler called the Coast Guard and claimed that Holloway had stepped out onto the deck for air that night, tripped and fell into the water. His boat mates later told investigators that they tried to save him by throwing him a lifeline, but it was all for naught; before he could reach the tube he was swept away by the turbulent waters of the gulf, six miles south of the Upper Matecumbe Key. The Coast Guard searched for his body for days with no luck. Without a body, even though he was pronounced dead, the insurance company would not allow Debbie to collect on the life insurance policy, a fact of which Holloway proudly stated he was aware.

The Coast Guard couldn't find the body for an obvious reason. Holloway was not really dead.

Zapone was freaking out when he heard of Holloway's death. Holloway had never told Zapone he was faking his death, but Zapone knew it had to be a hoax and he knew it was only a matter of time before investigators learned that he helped Holloway secure a loan and sell his two restaurants, money he said that Holloway obviously needed in order to disappear. He said he felt it was only a matter of time before the police called him, so he beat them to the punch. Within hours of hearing the news of Holloway's "death" he went to the police and told them that he believed Holloway was still alive.

Police told him that he had not provided them with any breaking news. They also knew it was a hoax and asked Zapone if they could tap his phone in case Holloway called. He agreed.

"I was covering my own ass," said Zapone. "I was not going to jail. I was innocent but you never know how a court will rule."

Hollow's son Daniel was in prison at the time for "petty crimes." He said he had not talked to his father for a while, but when investigators showed up at his cell and told him that his father had fallen off a boat and died he immediately knew it was a hoax. According to Daniel, his father often told people that if life ever got too tough he would simply fake his death, disappear for a while, take a much needed break and then reappear a few years later ready to start anew.

Investigators promised Daniel a reduced sentence if he could help lead them to his father. He said yes.

"He never did anything for me," said Daniel. "So I had no problem helping them out."

In exchange, investigators gave Daniel a new, much larger and solo cell with a police-tapped telephone. He was instructed to talk to as many people connected to his father as he could in hopes of one of them "spilling the beans." Daniel said about two months later his brother Randy was taped telling him that a friend of the family had told him that their dad was alive and well and living in Canada.

Holloway said that he left the pleasure cruise on September 3 and on the day he supposedly fell off the boat he was actually on a plane to New York with his new life insurance policy and a briefcase full of cash. He would not comment on how much he had, but investigators later stated that they believed he had over half a million dollars. Once in New York, he checked into Central Park's Wellington Hotel under the name James LaRue. In mid-October he crossed the border into Canada in a limousine with a girlfriend. A few weeks later, he sent her back to the United States. She smoked too much pot and he was afraid that she would bring unneeded attention upon him. Zapone said that Holloway never told him what happened in Canada, but a call he received one night may prove that he sent her home simply because he wanted to meet other women.

"I received the call around 7:30 p.m.," remembered Zapone. "It was a girl with a thick Canadian accent and she was asking me all sorts of questions about Gene. Did he really used to own a big restaurant in Tampa, was he really dead, and so on. It was about a three minute call, maybe two and a half minutes. I later came to find out that it was a girl in Canada he was trying to pick up. He was using his real story on her and he had her call me to confirm it. Unbelievable."

There was one woman he met, however, who did not know the true story until it was too late.

Gene Holloway Found Alive In Canada

Susan Wall was born and raised in Niagara. Except for trips to Toronto and a few other cities, she spent almost every day of her 25 years in the small town. That does not mean she was naïve. She was far from it. Niagara is a border town, after all, she explained, and shady characters passed through on a regular basis. She could tell a con man a mile away. Yet, when she met Holloway, she let her guard down.

She was sitting alone at the bar of the Thunder Bird Room, a then-popular Niagara watering hole known for its great live music, when she met him. She had met a lot of colorful characters in her life, but he was by far the most exotic. He was wearing his trademark cowboy hat and boots, along with a full-length suede coat with a fur collar. He told her his name was James LaRue and he was a seafood broker from Texas. He bought her drinks all night and, trying to impress her, he would tip the bartender $20 a drink. He was also obviously almost twice her age, despite his best efforts to hide his years behind hair dye. She said in retrospect she should have known he was full of BS, but he was so fascinating and exciting to be around that she fell for him.

"At the end of the night he gave me his phone number and told me that if I wanted to have dinner I should call him," remembered Wall. "And he told me I could bring whoever I wanted, except for boyfriends or husbands. For some reason I trusted him, but not enough to meet him alone. I brought my sister."

Both Wall and her sister missed further red flags during their dinner date with Holloway. He would tell stories about himself yet kept referring to himself as Gene rather than James LaRue.

"I thought he must have been telling stories that always included his friend Gene," laughed Wall. "I wondered why this guy Gene was always with him."

They c ontinued to date for a few weeks w ith Wall often bringing her sister along for the ride. W all s aid that after knowing one another for only two weeks, Holloway confided in her s ister that he was in love with Wall and would marry her. When her s ister told her the news, she was flattered but said she was not in love with him ... yet.

"I had feelings for h im," she s aid. "But love is a s trong emotion. I was excited, though. Here was a fascinating and successful man who was in love with me and kept promising me that he was returning to the U.S. one day and would bring me with him. It was an adventure."

A week after he expressed his love for her, he invited her to go to Toronto with him for an eye tuck. Holloway s aid he never received any p lastic s urgery, which W all s aid is p artially correct–an eye t uck i s n ot major enough t o be classified as "plastic surgery."

Holloway in Canada after faking his death

"It i s a v ery m inor procedure. He just had some lines he wanted taken care of," she s aid. "And he said when we left Toronto we were going skiing further north."

They had a blast in Toronto. They shopped all day at the finest stores and dined at night at the fanciest restaurants. For a man who was trying to convince the world he was dead, he was drawing a lot of attention to himself. Compounding matters, Holloway said he errantly chose his alias.

"Apparently, James LaRue was a wanted bandit in C anada," laughed Holloway. "Just my luck. Here I am, checking into a h otel as James LaRue and I give the hotel employees a big bag of cash to put in their safe. Pretty soon, the Royal Mounted Police took a room next to mine and began watching me."

The same l imousine d river who t ook Holloway across t he border was taking them to their ski destination. Wall said that she later learned Holloway had planned the ski trip with the girlfriend with whom he crossed the border into Canada. Before the limo driver left them, this ex-girlfriend had him promise to bring her more marijuana, which he did. He was not aware that Holloway sent that woman back to the Unites States. Wall said she was not a pot smoker and neither was Holloway at the time. Holloway said that when the limo driver handed Holloway the bag of marijuana, he wanted nothing to do with it so he placed it in a shoebox and hid it behind the vending machine down the hall, a move the police witnessed. It was all they needed to see. A man by the name of James LaRue had a ton of money in the hotel safe, was spending money loosely, and had a bag of marijuana. He was surely the infamous LaRue Canadian law enforcement had long wanted to arrest.

The next day, Wall and Holloway climbed into the limousine. Before the driver could exit the hotel's parking lot, the vehicle was swarmed by police and they arrested Holloway for drug trafficking. When they later fingerprinted Holloway they learned he was actually a man pronounced dead in the United States.

Wall was placed in an interrogation room with "a wall splattered in blood," she said, where she was informed of Holloway's true identity and story. She was not going to be charged with anything and the police would provide her with a ride home. She said that on her way out of the police station she saw Holloway sitting in an office with a few officers, laughing and having a ball as though nothing bad had happened.

"I got along fine with those officers," remembered Holloway. "They brought me a bottle of Jack Daniels at one point and we all had a few slugs. I stayed there for a few days and it was not bad at all. I then went to court in Canada and the judge told me he was going to transfer me back to the United States. I looked out into the court room audience and who do I see? I see all these news people from Tampa and around the country. I later found out that Johnny Carson mentioned me on his show."

Back in Tampa, the legend of Gene Holloway exploded unimaginably following the news that he was alive. He was the topic of seemingly every conversation. Songs were written about him and played on Tampa radio stations and local DJs hosted Gene Holloway look-alike contests. Ironically, the winner of WRBQ's was Ke nt McGregor, T ampa's l ead i nvestigator o n t he H olloway disappearance case.

"[McGregor] was later the best man at my wedding," laughed Z apone. "Life is funny."

Gene Holloway Goes To Jail

The trial changed him, said Wall. It brought him back down to earth, she claimed. It helped him realize that he had lost sight of reality and had gotten too caught up in the fast lane partying world.

What really drove that fact home was that his friends turned on him in the arson trial. The same people he supplied with endless fun for so many years took the stand and told the jury that he told them he burned down his Thonotosassa home.

Holloway said it did not bother him. He said his friends were only doing what they thought they needed to do. But W all who, despite H olloway's lies, moved to Tampa to be with Holloway after the arrest in Canada, said she thinks it did bother him.

"It wasn't just the trial," she said. "I think it became obvious to him that people were using him by the actions of friends who were not involved in the trial. We were living in a place on Busch Boulevard and people would stop by all day and n ight and t he first t hing t hey would d o is g o to his liquor cabinet and pour themselves a drink without even asking. They acted like they owned the place. Then we would go out to dinner with friends and none of them, not one, would pull out a wallet when the bill came. Gene always had to pay for everything."

On top of friends testifying that Holloway told them he was going to torch the house, the prosecution had investigators testify that Holloway's car was also lit on fire that night but before it was consumed someone removed its vanity plate that read, "Holloway."

Holloway's defense painted a picture of the witnesses being former friends who were angry with Holloway or who were paid by the prosecution to testify against him. The defense worked. Holloway was acquitted.

One juror told the daily newspaper reporters that the jury believed that Holloway was guilty, but they acquitted him because, "Nobody believed nobody," referencing the fact that the jury thought the prosecution was corrupt.

"The jury as a whole did not think the government gave sufficient evidence to prove Mr. Holloway was guilty beyond a reasonable doubt because of a conflict in evidence," the jury foreman was quoted as saying in daily newspapers following the acquittal.

Holloway was not clear yet. He still had to go on trial for conspiracy charges stemming from faking his own death. He said he could have beaten those charges as well, but chose to plead guilty and serve a five year sentence in order to remain alive. "There were still people trying to kill me," he said.

Before he disappeared from the public eye for half a decade, he gave reporters one last story. He met with reporters at his residence and explained why he faked his death. He said had been bored with his life and wanted to start anew so he could pursue adventure throughout the world. He even went into specifics, explaining that prior to faking his death he had been in contact with South African mercenaries who regularly frequented the Sea Wolf. He said they wanted his help with a coup attempt in Seychelles in the Indian Ocean and it was they who gave him the fake name James LaRue, told him to fake his death, and go to Canada to await their orders. Holloway said that following the coup attempt he was going to return to Tampa. He said he only set up the new life insurance policy in case he was killed in the coup.

"I'd rather not comment on that," said Holloway when asked if that story is true. "But I can tell you what is not true. A lot of people think I collected on that new life insurance policy. Well I did not. I never collected one penny on it. Print that please. I am tired of the lies. I could not collect on a policy that big without a body to show."

He served his sentence in Kentucky. Wall moved there and the two were married in 1982. She visited him almost every day of his incarceration. She said she saw firsthand how she believes prison changed him for the better. He began eating properly, she explained, exercising regularly and even ran marathons sponsored by the prison. He was a bright light in a dark place, she said, sponsoring

Christmas contests that gave prizes to the best decorated cell and he would help other prisoners better decorate their own cell by finding them things such as matching sheets for the beds.

"He would even scavenge around the prison for items he could turn into decorations for himself and others. I think he wanted to turn the prison into a Sea Wolf," she laughed.

Upon being released from prison, he opened three new Sea Wolfs between 1985 and 1990. One was located in a Best Western across from Busch Gardens. Another was in Hyde Park and the third was in Citrus County. He again tried to bring attention to them through outlandish PR stunts, such as hosting the Chippendale dancers.

Despite his best efforts, all three restaurants failed and he ended up in bankruptcy court in 1990.

"I never saw the originals," said Wall, "but I was with him for the second go around and from what I can tell from pictures I saw of the originals, he did not have the same money to put into the new ones. They were smaller and not as well decorated. I guess you can't recreate the past."

Wall said the number of hours he poured into trying to make the restaurants succeed placed too much stress on their marriage. Then, her mother became ill and she had to return to Canada. Shortly thereafter, they were divorced.

"He worked so much," she said. "He was the most driven man I had ever met and have not met anyone so hard working since. At times it was a detriment. I don't know if he always took the time to enjoy life. He was so consumed with being successful that the little things sometimes seemed unimportant to him."

When the success was gone, so were his many so-called friends. Without booze and parties to offer, they had no need for him anymore. Suddenly, Gene Holloway was alone ... and then, at some point in the 1990s, he disappeared and has rarely been heard from since.

Gene Holloway Today

He keeps quiet about what he is up to today. He likes to talk about treasure hunting and the skill that goes into it, but he is mum on his personal life.

He is an open book when reminiscing about the past but when the life of the present-day Gene Holloway is asked about, he clams up. His personal life is no longer public information. It is no longer a marketing weapon. His personal life is, well, it's personal.

He has no desire to return to the fast lane, he said. He has no desire to be the center of attention anymore, he promised. He enjoys the new simple life he has carved out for himself, he swears.

Following the closing of his last Sea Wolf in 1995, he relocated to Odessa and began his career as a treasure hunter along the coastline. He said treasure hunting had always been a dream but he was always so busy with making money that he did not take the time to pursue it.

He is also back in the food business. About eight years ago he noticed grocery stores throwing away food that was still safe for consumption. It was too old to sell but still fresh enough to eat. He began visiting every grocery and convenience store in the area, collecting the food and delivering it to homeless shelters, churches and soup kitchens in his area, anywhere that helps the needy.

Randy said that his father owes so much money to the federal government due to unpaid taxes and fines dating back to the 1980s and 90s that only a presidential pardon could free him of the debt.

Holloway seems honest when he says money means nothing to him anymore. He said he only wants to help his fellow man. To prove his sincerity, he said that his current treasure hunting mission is to find the legendary missing H-bomb that conspiracy theorists claim the U.S. government lost somewhere off the coast of Savannah, Georgia in the 1950s. Holloway said he is concerned that if it is not found, it could one day harm countless innocent people.

"I don't care about the fame," he said. "It's all about helping others now. It used to be about myself. Now I am least concerned with myself."

He sounded and looked earnest when he made that statement. But, then again ... he is Gene Holloway.

While Holloway was a genius when it came to keeping his name in the headlines, he paled in comparison to the true master of PR — Joe Redner.

Chapter 11
Six Feet of Fame: Joe Redner

Originally published in Cigar City Magazine Issue 26 in 2010

1972

      Empty beer bottles on a bar table rattle from the reverberations of the motorcycles pulling out of the parking lot outside. A beautiful blonde wearing nothing but a G-string and pasties hurtles a pile of swept up broken glass and hurries into the dressing room of the Deep South. A few more scantily clad dancers follow suit, all heading for the bar's dressing room so that they can grab their clothes and head home for the night.

The bouncers toss the straggling drinkers from the bar as the bartenders begin to clean up the night's mess. Smoke from smoldering cigarettes rise from beer bottles. Sticky, sugar-filled liquor drinks that were knocked over during a brief scuffle stain the bar, a few broken bottles from the fight have yet to be swept, and a dried pool of blood is caked to the floor. Tables are scattered about and chairs are everywhere; some are even turned upside down or on their backs.

One of the bar's owners, the 37-year-old Bobby Rodriguez, boasting slicked back hair, dusty jeans, sunglasses despite the late hour of the night, a tight black T-shirt, and swollen hands from years of crushing skulls, strolls through the bar and smiles at the carnage. A messy bar means a successful bar, and his bar has never enjoyed so much success. Business has doubled ever since his partner Pat Matassini hired some brash 32-year-old named Joe Redner to manage the bar eight months ago. Redner thought big. He came to the bar and saw that it was doing decent business with one stage and one go-go dancer performing at a time and decided that he would build two more stages so that three girls could dance at a time. His plan immediately saw dividends. More and more men flocked to the bar and it became one of Tampa's hottest nightspots.

Emerging from the dressing room of the bar with a fully-dressed dancer on his arm, Redner looks the part of a 70s swinger- thick mustache, flowery button-down shirt with a butterfly collar popping to the sides, wide bellbottoms and medium-length cropped hair. Jingling his motorcycle keys in his hands, he winks to Rodriguez and heads for the door, as the other dancers stare jealously at their coworker.

"Where the hell are you going?" asks Rodriguez in his raspy machismo voice. Rodriguez intimidates most men, but Redner, despite not being a fighter, doesn't flinch. Nothing seems to scare him.

"I'm going home," he says coolly and heads for the door.

"Not on my motorcycle you're not," screams Rodriguez.

"His motorcycle?" thinks Redner. "He gave me the motorcycle a few months ago as a present for my good work."

Rodriguez taps his own head with his forefinger. Redner knows what he is getting at.

"You're not going anywhere without a helmet," says an angry Rodriguez.

Without missing a beat, Redner reaches behind the bar, grabs an ice bucket, places it on the girl's head and leaves the bar.

Rodriguez rushes out of the bar to tell Redner to get his butt back inside, but Redner is already pulling out of the parking lot, the dancer holding him tightly around the waist- the ice bucket on her head and a helmet on his.

Seated left is Bobby Rodriquez with associates.

"He was a crazy son of a bitch," laughed Rodriguez while reminiscing about the night in an interview published in *La Gaceta* in 2007. "Crazy and stubborn."

These two attributes are what enabled Joe Redner, a high school dropout, to later become a self made millionaire and one of the most well-known adult business owners in the country. Redner didn't invent nudity, but he did invent nude clubs in Tampa and he made these bars as much a part of Tampa's lure as *café con leche* and cigars.

But, in December 1999, Redner's empire was threatened. In the process his name transcended the strip club industry and he became more than "the strip club king," he became one of the most infamous men in Tampa; its loveable outlaw.

At issue was Tampa City Council's 1999 attempt to ban lap dancing in the city. If the ban was enacted, Redner, the godfather of Tampa strip clubs, said his establishments would have gone bankrupt. The City Council said they wanted the dances banned because they promoted prostitution and spread disease. Redner claimed City Council was trying to regulate morality. When the two sides went to war, an epic battle ensued, a war that was talked about in every corner of the nation.

Born in Hackensack, NJ in 1940 to Richard and Agnes Redner, Joe Redner moved to Tampa at the age of 8 with his mother following his parents' divorce. By his sophomore year of high school, he said he realized that school was not for him, and dropped out.

"I always felt out of place," Redner told the *St. Petersburg Times* in a profile published on January 21, 1991. "I didn't laugh at the same things. I didn't like the same things. I just couldn't remember things, you know. Other kids would get A's in spelling without even trying. I'd study and study and still not pass. It just didn't seem fair."

In the ensuing years, he bounced around from job to job, including five years in the carnival business. He then moved to Illinois and married an exotic dancer. While she danced, Redner worked as a bouncer. Eventually, they divorced. Redner married wife number two soon after, but that also ended in divorce. He returned to Tampa and picked up where he left off- working odd jobs where he could find them. He worked in a furniture store. He started his own business maintaining parking lots.

In the early 1970s, he performed some carpentry work for Pat Matassini. Matassini owned a number of bars in Tampa, including the Pad Lounge- a popular music venue- and the Deep South, Tampa's first go-go bar. Matassini and Redner became friends and Matassini hired him to work the door at the Pad Lounge. When a manager's position became available at the Deep South, he gave it to Redner, believing that Redner's hardworking attitude would have a good affect on the bar. He was right. Redner built new stages for the bar, hired more beautiful women to dance, and turned it into the place to be. After a few years, Redner felt he was ready to make the move from management to ownership.

In 1975, while listening to the radio on a drive home from the Deep

South, Redner heard a news report that would change his life and the city of Tampa forever. The United States Supreme Court had ruled that drive-in movie theaters could show films with nudity because movies constituted free speech, which is protected under the First Amendment. A light went off in Redner's head. He had long thought that if women in G-strings and pasties were drawing a crowd, women wearing absolutely nothing would draw enormous crowds. He rationalized that if nudity in a movie wasn't obscene because it constituted free speech, then a nude dance shouldn't be obscene either because it was also a form of entertainment and artistic expression.

In 1976, Redner decided to test his assessment of the Supreme Court ruling and venture out on his own. He opened Tampa's first all nude club- the Night Gallery. Redner was right- men flocked to his establishment. The city leaders, though, didn't agree with his legal argument that nude dancers were constitutionally protected- they deemed them obscene. The city asked the Hillsborough County Court to declare Redner's club illegal because it was a "house of ill fame," and threatened to arrest Redner and the dancers if he didn't have the women wear at least G-strings and pasties.

The stubborn Redner, a high school dropout from a blue collar family who was making more money than he had ever dreamt he'd make, refused to comply with the city's wish.

"I wasn't open one week before they started raiding me," said Redner in the 2008 documentary on his life, *Strip Club King*. "And then they started raiding me five days a week, and only because the vice squad didn't work on Sundays and Mondays. And then it got to the point that they were raiding me seven or eight times a day."

Redner said the Tampa Police Department would send an undercover police officer to the Night Gallery. The officer would take a seat at the bar and wait for each girl to dance. Once the rotation of girls was complete, the officer would identify himself and arrest all the girls. With no girls to dance, Redner would have to shut down for the night.

To combat the police, Redner began breaking up his girls into shifts- three girls per rotation. When a rotation was over and the police would arrest the girls, Redner would send the second shift up. When they were arrested, he'd send a third shift. And by the time they were arrested, the first shift would be bailed out and ready to take the stage again. Redner paid for the fines, and the girls were making so much money that the hassle was worth it.

Emboldened by his success, along with his former boss, Bobby Rodriguez, Redner opened a second all-nude club, the Tanga Lounge. The police used the same method to raid the new bar and Redner used the same methods to combat it.

In the early 1980s, the Florida Supreme Court declared that the charges against Redner—that he ran a " house of ill fame" and that his dancers worked at one- were unconstitutional, stating that the phrase "house of ill fame" was such an antiquated term that it was meaningless. Believing he was now free to operate without city interference, in 1982 Redner opened a third bar- Mons Venus. But the city's war against Redner had only just begun. The Florida Supreme Court ruled that city governments had the right to revoke a bar's liquor license if the city deemed the bar a nuisance. Tampa immediately took away his clubs' liquor licenses, but not even this move could stop Redner. He knew that the women, not alcohol, were his main draw. He remained open, making his money off cover charges, bottled water and non-alcoholic beer. Redner claimed the Mons Venus actually improved after he ceased selling alcohol, as sober patrons meant calmer and more respective patrons.

Nude clubs were now popping up all over Tampa as Redner's victories over the city gave others the courage to open similar businesses. The city was quickly becoming known as the "strip club capitol of the world."

Believing the city would turn into a strip club amusement park if they didn't act, in 1982 the city leaders passed a zoning ordinance disallowing sexually oriented businesses from opening within 500 feet of any property zoned for residential or office use and at least 1,000 feet from another adult-oriented business. Mons Venus and the Tanga Lounge were both in violation of this new zoning law due to being located too close to office space, so Redner filed a law suit against the city of Tampa, claiming that the new zoning ordinances were unconstitutional.

Not only did his lawsuit allow his clubs to remain open while the court debated the zoning ordinance, but Redner continued to expand his empire. He was fought every step of the way.

In 1984, he tried to open a nude club on Seventh Avenue in Ybor City, but the city declined his business license, citing an earlier drug conviction as the reason. Redner sued the city in federal court, won a $1,000 settlement and the court ruled that the city had to license his club. The club later closed anyway due to lack of business.

In 1988, Redner planned to open a nude club in Citrus County, but just days before he was set to open the doors the Citrus County Commission held an emergency meeting adopting a temporary ordinance that established new rules and regulations for operating adult businesses in Citrus County. Redner opened the club anyway, believing it was unconstitutional for him to be punished by laws put into place after he announced he was opening a business.

The girls danced, the police came, everyone was arrested, the county shut down the bar, and Redner sued the county. In 1992, the U.S. District Court for the Middle District of Florida ruled that the ordinance was indeed unconstitutional. The judge said that while nude dancing is subject to governmental regulation, Citrus County's ordinance went too far because it didn't promise a quick appeal if a license was denied, meaning the County Commission could stall the procedure indefinitely. Redner was awarded a $374,000 settlement against Citrus County. Despite the victory, he decided against reopening the club.

While the Citrus County case played out, Redner was also suing Hillsborough County. In March 1990, he opened Mons II in an area of unincorporated Hillsborough County. A week after he opened, the county filed an injunction ordering him to shut down. The County Commission claimed that Mons II was too close- 1,000 feet- to the Florida Suncoast Gymnastics Academy, which also served as a kindergarten, violating a county zoning ordinance disallowing adult oriented establishments from operating within 2,000 feet of churches, schools or parks. Redner shut down the club but filed a lawsuit against the county, claiming that the county never properly advertised the ordinance as a rezoning proposal and that the school in question was hastily organized after he decided to open his club. In November 1991, Hillsborough County Circuit Judge Richard Lazzara ruled in favor of Redner. A federal jury later awarded him $230,000 in damages and he never reopened the club.

Redner was winning more than money in each lawsuit he filed; he was winning over the people.

All of the free publicity turned the Mons Venus into the most popular nude club in the city and one of the most famous in the world. "The Mons Venus has achieved legendary status within America's sex trade," wrote Steve Huettel in a 1999 profile on Redner in the *St. Petersburg Times*. He then reported that the Mons Venus yielded Redner "an impressive profit: roughly $1 million a year on revenues of $3 million. (That money is nearly all from the club's cover charges; it does not include what the dancers earn.) His half interest in the Tanga Lounge is worth $300,000 annually."

Tampa City Council and Redner then butted heads in 1996 when Redner opened a nude club, Club Flamingo, on Seventh Avenue in Ybor City. The move threatened the future of the Centro Ybor project, a development city leaders hoped would revive a struggling historic district.

"Our prospective customers are national retailers," Jay Miller, executive vice president of Steiner Associates, was quoted as saying in a December 1999 *Tampa Tribune* article. Steiner Associates was the developer of Centro Ybor.

"We expressed concern to the mayor that the destination would become more slanted towards adult entertainment."

"I went to Joe and I told him that the developers wouldn't build Centro Ybor if there was a strip club down the road," said then- Mayor Dick Greco. "I told him the city couldn't afford to lose Centro Ybor, but he didn't care. He told me to sue him if I didn't like it."

The city did take Redner to court and it had the ammunition it needed to win.

In early 1996, after 14 years of court battles, U.S. District Court Judge Susan Bucklew upheld the city's 1982 zoning ordinance, stating that the zoning restrictions still allowed adult oriented businesses in three parts of the city- those zoned for general, intense and heavy industrial- and that 72 sites totaling 5,364 acres remained available for adult oriented businesses. Because Redner's Club Flamingo was within 1,000 feet of office space, it was illegally zoned, which gave the city the right to shut it down.

The city filed a lawsuit in Hillsborough County Court in April 1996 against 10 strip clubs that violated the zoning ordinance. The city asked the judge to fine each club $1,000 per day until they shut down. Club Flamingo wasn't the only Redner-owned club named in the lawsuit. So was Mons Venus, the bread and butter of his enterprise.

"I never intended to close Mons Venus," said Greco. "I just didn't want a strip club in Ybor City. I didn't want it to stop us from getting Centro Ybor done. But the city couldn't file a lawsuit against just one club; they all had to be included. If Joe had just not opened Club Flamingo, the suit would never have been filed." Greco promised the Centro Ybor developers that Club Flamingo would soon be gone, and the development went on as planned.

In January 1999, Hillsborough County Circuit Court Judge James Moody ruled that Club Flamingo was violating the zoning ordinance and had to cease nude dancing. Redner abided by the decision, but the court ruled that all clubs that opened prior to the 1982 ordinance, such as Mons Venus and the Tanga Lounge, were allowed to stay open because a business cannot be "retroactively punished." By successfully shutting down Club Flamingo, the city won a battle against Redner, but the war was far from over.

In 1999, Redner ran for Tampa City Council with a campaign theme focused on his years of long legal battles with city and county governments. He argued that Tampa needed a leader who would fight for the rights of business and property owners, claiming that Tampa was becoming "Big Brother."

Redner's opponent was a perfect foil- Bob Buckhorn, an incumbent who spent his first four years on the council as its spokesperson against indecency. Buckhorn drafted an ordinance banning "rave clubs," all night establishments that catered to patrons of all ages and that had a reputation for allowing open drug use. He also railed against prostitution with three ordinances that, according to a 1999 profile on Buckhorn by *St. Petersburg Times* reporter Steve Huettel, "alarmed some civil libertarians. He pushed for an ordinance to impound the cars of people arrested for soliciting prostitutes and put their pictures on government-access television. Buckhorn also proposed making it a crime to flash undercover cops or make them expose themselves, which was a common tactic for prostitutes. And he advocated tougher enforcement against lingerie modeling shops, massage parlors and body scrub shops, targeted by police as fronts for prostitution. Buckhorn wears those crusades against sex and drugs like battle medals."

Redner's supporters depicted him as the last line of defense against an increasingly oppressive city government. Buckhorn's supporters depicted him as the man fighting for Tampa's family values.

In the end, the election wasn't close. In March 1999, Buckhorn defeated Redner by a 3-1 ratio. The resounding defeat wasn't about to dampen Redner's longtime fight against what he deemed to be oppressive governments. If anything, in defeat he actually won, as his campaign made national news- the sex peddler running for office. The election increased his fame and strengthened his reputation as an anti-establishment leader.

Ironically, while the adult-business zoning ordinance allowed the city to keep nude clubs out of the areas the administration's development efforts were focused on, specifically Ybor City and Channelside, it caused problems in Drew Park, an area of Tampa located on the outskirts of the Tampa International Airport.

"In the late 1980s, Drew Park residents lobbied for blanket commercial zoning, in an effort to keep their property values high. They believed the Tampa Aviation Authority would soon be buying up land to expand the airport," wrote *Tampa Tribune* reporter David Pedreira in 1997. " They ended up getting expansion of a different kind."

Adult clubs and massage parlors flocked to the area when their owners realized they wouldn't face the usual distance requirements from homes and churches. By the late 1990s, almost 20 adult businesses were located in the small community, and the residents began complaining to the city that some of the strip clubs and massage parlors were peddling more than nudity. They were selling drugs and prostitutes.

"When someone asks me where I live, I'm embarrassed to tell them," one resident told Pedreira for his *Tribune* article. "It's just unreal what's happening."

The city vowed to crack down on prostitution throughout the city, a measure made increasingly possible after Buckhorn's anti-prostitution laws were passed. In 1997, police made more than 1,000 prostitution arrests. In June 1998, police raided more than 20 massage parlors, body scrub salons and lingerie shops, arresting 36 people on charges ranging from prostitution and drugs to illegally performing massages. That year, 39 licensed body scrub shops were reclassified under bathhouse codes, forcing workers to apply for a license, take a 70-hour course on the theory of bathing and wear surgical gowns when bathing clients. In 1996, more than 70 massage parlors and lingerie modeling studios existed. Two years later, only 18 remained.

The strip clubs in Drew Park remained a problem, though. Undercover police reported to the city that strippers in some Drew Park strip clubs would take men into VIP rooms for private lap dances and perform oral sex for extra money, while bolder clubs allowed the strippers to have sex with men right out in the open while the other patrons watched.

"Lap dancing was becoming more than lap dancing in these clubs," said Greco. "The more prominent ones like Mons Venus were fine. Joe always ran clean places. But some of the ones in Drew Park were terrible."

"Sure these places are on the sleazy side and they don't help the neighborhood," City Councilman Charlie Miranda was quoted as saying in the *St. Petersburg Times* in 1997. "But if the zoning for adult businesses is there, which it is, there's really not much we can do."

Then, City Council did find something they could do. They took a cue from Hillsborough County's neighbor- Pinellas County.

In the early 1990s, in order to crack down on the county's prostitution problem, Pinellas County passed a law prohibiting strip club patrons from being within three feet of the dancers. It solved Pinellas County's problem, but added to Tampa's, as unhappy customers flocked to Tampa where strip clubs, according to the Pinellas County Sheriff's Office, were "more of a free for all."

In September 1999, the Tampa City Council announced they would be voting on an ordinance in December that would forbid strip club patrons from being within six-feet of the strippers, criminalizing lap dances. Violators would face a maximum penalty of $1,000 and six months in jail. Establishments with more than three violations in 30 days could be declared a public nuisance and the city could go to court to shut them down. City Council also claimed the lap dance ban would help cut down on STDs, which they claimed were spread by lap dances.

Redner didn't see the ordinance as a health issue or as a way to stop the shadier strip clubs from dealing in prostitution. He saw it as a danger to the empire he'd built. If lap dances were banned, he thought his clubs would go out of business. People went to his club specifically for lap dances, not to watch strippers get naked six feet away. Following City Council's announcement of the pending vote, Redner announced he would spend millions of dollars to fight the six-foot rule.

"If Joe had never made a big deal out of it, I don't think we ever would have bothered his clubs," said Greco. "This was about cracking down on clubs breaking the law. Joe's clubs were fine. The police probably never would have said anything to him if he kept allowing lap dances had he not turned it into such a big issue."

In the two months leading up to the vote on the ordinance, Redner led an all-out public relations war on the Tampa City Council.

Strip club owners collected thousands of signatures for petitions that they sent to the city. And dancers went public with their stories, telling the media that their wages enabled them to raise their children and send them to private schools they wouldn't be able to afford with other jobs. The quadriplegic brother of a dancer at Mons Venus told the press that without his sister's income to help him with his bills, he'd have to move into a nursing home.

Redner bought full-page ads in newspapers stating that sexual oppression is unhealthy and that the city had no right to regulate morality. He hired lobbyists to help him with his campaign and paid economists to put together an economic study touting the impact strips clubs had on the city. According to the study, the clubs had a $110 million a year impact on the city through the wages of the 6,000 jobs the industry created. Redner also preached that some conventions chose Tampa specifically because of its numerous strip clubs.

"These clubs probably outdraw the Buccaneers and Devil Rays

combined," wrote St. Petersburg Times reporter Howard Troxler on September 19, 1999, following the release of the economic impact report. "A few years ago, the taxpayers built a $30 million stadium for the New York Yankees on the excuse that their spring training games would produce an economic impact of $50 million a year. By that logic, shouldn't we be offering to build Redner a bigger place?"

Escalating the war of words was Buckhorn, who became the City Council's spokesman for the six-foot ordinance, appearing before the cameras as often as Redner, continuing to proclaim that nude clubs promoted prostitution and STDs. Despite the fact that Redner's clubs were not the ones promoting prostitution, Buckhorn wasn't distinguishing Redner's clubs from the guilty ones, furthering the illusion that the six-foot ban was a personal crusade by the city against Redner.

"Bob saw it as his way to become mayor," said one City Hall insider who did not want to be named. "He thought it was his ticket to the mayor's office. He thought it was the issue that would get his name out there. He even had six-foot rulers made up with his name on them. He turned it into a moral issue, not a political issue."

"Once Bob Buckhorn got involved in it, it really got big," said a member of the city's legal department, who also wished to remain anonymous. "He didn't initiate that thing. The legal department was already working on it, but he was so vocal about it that he got the credit for it. Bob meant well, but I don't think he ever gave a good explanation on why we were passing it. It was being done to end the prostitution in Drew Park. But Bob got caught up in a war of words with Joe, so the reason behind the law was lost, and in the process Bob helped turn Joe into a cult hero."

Churches and congregations got involved, picketing outside strip clubs, and gathering tens of thousands of signatures and placing full-page ads in newspapers on behalf of the lap dance ban.

Redner and his crusade against the city even made national headlines and news programs, including *20/20* and *The Daily Show*. He was usually billed as a hero, a man fighting against the prudish Tampa City Council members who wanted to regulate the city's morality.

On *The Daily Show*, Redner joked that the only way a blind man knew what the dancers looked like was by feeling them like brail. The segment ended with *The Daily Show's* host, Jon Stewart, asking, "What kind of monsters would pass a law that would hurt blind men?"

"There's more interest in this than in any election I've ever seen," Tampa City Councilman Charlie Miranda told the St. Petersburg Times prior to the December 2, 1999 lap dance ban vote. "They're aware of the issue and what's going on. It's sad in a way."

The City Council vote had to be moved from City Hall to the Convention Center. Over 2,000 people attended. The meeting began at 1 p.m. and didn't end until 2 a.m., as countless individuals with signs verbally attacking City Council, and national news cameras were all over the city. In the end, city leaders would not bow to public pressure. Following a unanimous vote by City Council, the six-foot ordinance was signed into law.

As he always did, Redner fought back. He publicly stated that the dancers would continue to offer lap dances. He hung signs from the Mons Venus taunting Greco- "Dicky Greco the New Morality God," "Hey Greco. Censor This," "Hey Mayor. Come in and Enforce Your Ordinance," and "Mayor Greco and His Looney Tune Police Dept. are a Joke." He stood in front of Mons Venus, hordes of press from around the country filming and snapping pictures, and gave fiery speeches about how he would not allow Greco and City Council to regulate morality and trample on his First Amendment rights.

"I'm not going to stop anything," he told Tampa's Fox News. "I'm not going to stop anything until the mayor comes in and shoots me."

"He even put the phone numbers for city councilmen on his signs outside his club," said an anonymous City Hall insider. "And people would drive by and see it and call. We'd leave the office in the evening and by the time we went to work in the morning our voice mail was full...Some people left real nasty messages... We were even getting calls from all over the country. I remember getting one from Arizona from a woman asking why we were banning lap dances. It was absolutely crazy."

Redner filed suit against the city, stating that one of the reasons behind the ordinance- that lap dances promote sexually transmitted diseases- could not be proven. Redner also pledged to bail out any dancer who was arrested and said that if the city filed charges against the dancers he would counter sue for violation of their First Amendment rights.

The press continued to rally behind Redner.

"Mayor D ick Greco and the Tampa City Council look ridiculous for wasting so much time, and so many c ity resources, in t heir c rusade to b an lap dancing," editorialized the *St. Petersburg Times* on December 4, 1999.

"Did I miss s omething here?" wondered *The Tampa Tribune's* Dan Ruth in a column he wrote on January 19, 2001. "Have I s uddenly a wakened t o find myself living in Amish country with John Ashcroft as the mayor?"

"Joe i s a s mart man," s aid Greco. "He m ade it seem like t he city was waging a war on h im and only h im... he knew if he fought it, he would get more free press, which meant more people would go to his club."

Despite Redner being a thorn in the city's s ide, the police did not bother the Mons Venus for six months after the ordinance was passed.

At a p olitical function in July 2000, Redner and Greco crossed paths for the first time s ince the ordinance was passed. Greco tried to s hake Redner's hand. Redner refused t o do s o, t elling the mayor t hat t hey were not friends, they were enemies.

"And he told me, 'Well, then let's go to war,'" s aid Redner. Greco denied ever saying that.

A week after their encounter at the church, the Mons Venus was raided for the first time. Greco denied to the press that the raid had anything to do with his meeting with Redner, b ut was a ctually planned for a month. Raids the s ize of the one on Mons Venus are not planned in a week, he explained, but actually takes months to put together. Police raided five clubs over a two-day period, arresting 46 women and 33 men, all charged with b reaking the six-foot o rdinance. Over the next few months, raids were a regular occurrence.

Redner continued to openly allow lap dances, and began employing the same method to keep dancers on stage as he used decades ago- one set of dancers would be arrested and the next set would take the stage.

"The six foot law wasn't doing anything but putting innocent people in jail temporarily. At one point I saw that 135 dancers were arrested for violating that stupid law," said Redner. "Each hearing would take half a day to a day, and if any were granted a jury trial, they would take even longer. The prosecutors offered a deal- $200 in fines and six months' probation and blah, blah, blah, blah and they wouldn't put anyone in jail... I said we want to try every case. On top of that, I demanded a speedy trial for every one of them, which meant they had 90 days to try each case or have to throw them out. There was no way they were going to be able to do that, especially when the judge had his normal case load to handle, including a ton of DUIs. So the prosecution gave up. They let the dancers plead no contest, pay no fine or court costs, withheld adjudication and gave the dancers no probation. So basically they were treated like jaywalkers."

In August 2001, the ordinance took a major legal hit when Hillsborough County Circuit Judge Elvin Martinez signed an order declaring the ordinance unconstitutional, saying it was too broad and allowed selective enforcement and that lap dancing was not a risk to public health or safety.

"Statutes or ordinances cannot be so overbroad that they prohibit constitutionally protected conduct as well as unprotected conduct," wrote Martinez. "They also cannot be so overbroad they make common conduct criminal and provide the police with unfettered discretion to arrest."

"The judge also found practical problems with the ordinance, 'considering the realities of movement' inside a strip club. For example, someone could be guilty for passing by an unclothed person on the way to the restroom. Furthermore, the city failed to prove that the ordinance 'furthers a substantial government interest,' reported the *St. Petersburg Times* on August 2, 2001.

Following Martinez's ruling, the six-foot ordinance faded away. It was never removed from the books as law, but it was never enforced again. The legacy of the six-foot rule, though, will perhaps never fade away.

Just as the lap dance war came to an end, another battle involving nudity erupted and Tampa was once again thrust into the national spotlight.

Chapter 12
White Chocolate vs Ronda Storms

Charles Perkins aka White Chocolate the faux pimp who hosted the raunchy White Chocolate Show.

Countless men and woman have the "Public Access Rags to Riches" dream. Cut their teeth in the low budget studio. Earn a small fan base in the city. Get discovered and turn into a national superstar. Unfortunately, the list of those who have made that leap is short. Max Kellerman parlayed a New York City public access show into a successful career as an ESPN analyst and a boxing commentator.

Tom Green hosted a public access variety show in Ottawa before he was discovered by MTV.

And that may be it in terms of recent Public Access personalities who made it big.

In 2002, for a brief time, it appeared that Tampa had a Public Access personality ready to add his name to the list–Charles Perkins, a ka White Chocolate, the faux pimp who hosted the raunchy "White Chocolate Show" that broadcast such controversial footage as women fondling themselves in showers, a stick puppet of an African American county commissioner being hung by a tree and a sock puppet offering a female county commissioner puppet sexual favors.

He lived his pimp gimmick 24/7, wearing his trademark fur coat, gold chains and pimp hat almost everywhere he went. He was a regular guest on a local FM radio station. He was invited to appear on nationally broadcast daytime talk shows. He opened his own Ybor City nightclub. He even had a bevy of girlfriends who were his Public Access groupies by day and dancers at some of Tampa's most frequented strip clubs by night. They were the type of woman whose looks could have landed them doctors or lawyers. But they instead chose to sleep on the couch of a man who at times dressed like a nun and played with Osama bin Laden puppets.

"It was crazy. When it began, I never thought it would become as big as it did. Most of the time, it was all a joke to me but people kept watching and talking about it, saying good things and bad things. It was the bad things that fueled me. They kept feeding it and the more bad things they said the further I wanted to push it. I was just having fun getting under people's skin and trying to prove the point that free speech means free speech," explained Charles Perkins.

The more he pushed the boundaries of decency, the more Tampa Bay talked about him. His show drew the ire or applause of seemingly everyone in Tampa Bay and turned the community into a national battlefield in the free speech vs. obscenity debate, launching himself into local stardom, a little-talked-about county commissioner into a national p olitical c elebrity, a nd T ampa's r arely watched Public A ccess Channel into one of the most viewed stations in all of the city.

"I was just a kid really," s aid a more mature Perkins o f h is 25-year-old self. Today, he is a 36-year-old loyal husband and father who has long s ince turned in the fur coat and pimp hat. "And I was taking advantage of my moment I guess. But I'm not that guy anymore. "

He is not that guy AT ALL. The young man who would search for ways to make the headlines for all the wrong reasons is now trying to make the headlines for all the right ones. White Chocolate is trying to launch a career in politics, h oping to win a s eat on e ither the Tampa City Council or Hillsborough County Commission so he can help rebuild his deteriorating neighborhood in North Tampa.

"Drive through and around the neighborhoods in the Armenia Avenue and 50th Street area," he said. "Some of the neighborhoods don't have sidewalks. Other neighborhoods don't even have paved roads. It's 2011 and they still have dirt roads. That is ridiculous. Meanwhile, the city keeps giving more and more money to the rich over in New Tampa. How is this fair?"

He has run for political office twice so far and has come up short each time but vows to continue to run until he wins. And he said that when he DOES win, he will not keep one penny of the salary. He will instead donate it back to the community.

"Helping your community is not a job," he said. "It is a privilege. I don't want to be a career politician. I don't want to use a seat in office as a spring board to other political jobs. I just want to help my neighborhood."

There was no smirk or roll of the eyes when he made that comment. Charles Perkins, "White Chocolate" himself, was actually 100 percent serious. He no longer seems to care about obtaining 15 minutes of fame. He actually seems to care about his community. But, despite his seemingly earnest intentions, the million dollar question is, "Can a man who once dressed like a pimp and showed footage of women masturbating in the shower while he read children's stories win an election?"

"Of course I can," he snapped. "Because I am real. I am who I am. When a voter recognizes me, I don't deny who I am or who I was. But I do tell them that I am not that guy anymore and when I tell them what I want to do for their neighborhood they see me as a leader and not a public access pimp. Look, you can't go through life with regrets. I don't regret what I did or who I was. It is what it is.

"Look man. Before you can become the man you want to be you have to accept the man who you were," he continued, taking a breath to grin in a sign of self-acknowledgement of his profound statement. "I know who I was and I am not ashamed of it or anything about my life. I am an open book. I have nothing to hide. I'll tell you whatever you want to know about me."

And he did. For the first time ever, he shed the "White Chocolate" costume and allowed someone to see Charles Perkins – the man he is, the man he was, and the man he still wants to become.

"I'm deep," he joked. "Real deep."

Perkins was born on November 10, 1975 and was raised an only child behind Chamberlain High School on the corner of Busch Boulevard and Linebaugh Avenue.

His parents divorced when he was 5 years old, but he stayed close with his father during his formative childhood years.

"My father was my hero," said Perkins. "He was a real hero, a World War II hero."

According to Perkins, his father's battalion had to storm a German pillbox located on the top of a hill. Everyone in the battalion but his father and one other soldier were killed shortly into the offensive. His father did not back down, however. He instead charged the hill, spraying the Germans with bullets. When he ran out of ammo he picked up a shovel and beat the Germans manning the pillbox to death, successfully completing the mission.

"I swear it's true," said Perkins. "I have seen letters and newspaper articles about it. I was always proud of him for that. He stood up for something great. I just wanted to be around him all the time when I was a kid."

In order to spend time with his father, he often accompanied him to work.

His father's clients, however, were not the type a young boy should have been around.

"He built secret rooms inside of houses for mobsters and bikers who lived in Carrollwood and Ybor City," said Perkins. "These were known guys. They would have a fake wall in a den or living room and when you pressed a button the wall would open up and reveal the hidden room my father built."

Perkins' father taught him everything he knew and as the years progressed, Perkins graduated from a simple helper to his father's full-fledged apprentice. Then, when Perkins was around 12 or 13 years old, he and his father had a falling out and have not spoken since.

"I think he may be dead," said Perkins. "I don't care where he is or what happened to him. When I was in junior high, I overheard him on the phone with my mom saying something like, 'I think our son would kill me in his sleep if he had the chance.' I have no idea why he said that but I was crushed. I looked up to my father. When I heard him say something so terrible about me it broke me and I never spoke to him again."

But, he did keep the lessons he taught him.

With his mother working fulltime, Perkins had little parental supervision as a teenager. He used this freedom to become THE party guy at his high school by building an underground party room in his backyard, mimicking those secret rooms he used to build with his father. He said the room was a work of art, complete with hard wood floors and cubbyholes in the walls for alcohol storage.

Alcohol was something easy for him to get his hands on. He also made and sold fake IDs. Every weekend he would put on a lab coat, rub some black makeup under his nose to create a five o'clock shadow on his upper lip, clip a USF medical student ID he made at home onto the jacket, and purchase alcohol using his fake ID at a liquor store drive thru. He would then return to the underground room in his backyard and host the weekend's best party. Because the room had limited space, it was an invite only party with guests clamoring to go. By the end of the party, bodies were strewn across the hidden room's floor and the smell of vomit was overpowering.

"My mom knew I had the room," explained Perkins. "There was no way to hide it from her when I was building it, but she thought it was just a boy's clubhouse. She had no way of knowing what really went on. Then one weekend when I was at a Saturday morning detention she saw one of my friends passed out on the lawn and when she checked on him she looked into the room for the first time and saw what we really did. When I got home, she made me cave the room in."

Perkins refused to allow that to be the end of his partying ways. At the age of 15, using his fake IDs, he rented a townhome near the University of South Florida. By that point he had earned and saved quite a bit of money by selling the fake IDs and by working at a KB Toy Store. He paid for the entire year's lease up front, enabling him to avoid a credit and background check. And because the rental home was near a popular college, police left his parties alone, thinking it was another college party rather than a high school kegger.

The parties featured plenty of beer, a two-story funnel, and a pool of beer on the first floor that partiers dove into from the second floor. At the end of each party, he cleaned and then returned to his mother's house.

"It was just a party house," he said. "I didn't live there."

He rented the townhome throughout high school. Following graduation, he had little desire to attend college. He knew what he wanted to do – run his own business. Because he made a profit off the fake IDs and parties, coupled with the fact that he'd become a manager at KB Toy Store, he felt he had the experience and know-how.

His first legal business venture was a Saturn Subs in what was then the East Lake Mall. His calling card was a one-dollar hotdog and soda. The business was a success in terms of moving products, but it was not providing him with the type of income he wanted.

He sold the business for a small profit and returned to KB Toy Store for a few years before again venturing out on his own, this time opening Cheap Auto Repair on East Hillsborough Avenue. Perkins knew next to nothing about fixing cars, but he knew commerce. On that strip of road on Hillsborough Avenue were a car lot and auto shop but no auto repair shop. He knew there was a need for one. He hired a handful of qualified mechanics and was open for business.

Perkins also knew how to promote, bringing in customers with unique promotions that catered to that area's low income clientele. For instance, covering one side of his building was his slogan, "We have crack head prices!"

"There was a ton of crack heads in that area," laughed Perkins. "And they would come by the shop all the time with random objects they were trying to sell, like DVD players and pairs of shoes. I wouldn't want anything they were selling, but they were persistent. They would say the DVD player was $5 and I'd say no. So they'd drop it to $3 and I'd still say no. Finally they would offer it to me for a buck, so of course I had to take it at that price. I even had one crack head who stopped by with a pair of scissors and asked to cut the lawn. I didn't even have a real lawn; it was just one strip of grass, but I said sure and offered to pay him $10. When I checked in on him, he was cutting my grass with the scissors. It was crazy. So that is what crack head prices meant – we were always willing to negotiate and would do anything to get your business, like a crack head. The people in that community understood it and loved the slogan."

His other famous promotion was "Pimp Discount Mondays." He offered a 30 percent discount to anyone who looked like a pimp, whether they were a real pimp or fake. More often than not, however, the pimps were real. The promotion was such a hit he decided to run with it. He would wear a fur coat and pimp hat, stand on the corner of the road near his shop, and wave a sign to the passersby that read either "We Have Crack Head Prices" or "Pimp Discount Mondays."

"And that's how my pimp character was born," he said.

Perkins was a teenager, 13 or 14, when he bought his first video camera. He and his friends would hide with it near the fairways of a local golf course. When a ball rolled by, Perkins would grab it and film the golfers' reactions when they couldn't find the ball. If the golfer saw him grab the ball and run, the reaction was even funnier, explained Perkins

He also filmed his own comedy skits. In one of his earliest creations, he played a Russian chef who prepared his dishes with a chainsaw. Unfortunately, his Russian accent was the only thing worse than the production value, he admitted. He knew he had the creative mind it took to entertain. What he needed was the skill. This is where Public Access entered the picture.

Sometime a round 1 990, h e w as c hannel s urfing one night when he stumbled upon footage of beautiful girls flashing their breasts at Tampa's various beer-soaked parades. The s how, *Lifestyles of the Up and Coming*, was ca using quite a stir in Tampa Bay at the time. Conservative politicians and church leaders said it was pornography and was exploiting drunken girls who did not know their half-naked images would end u p on television. The s how's s upporters u sed the First A mendment to defend it. In t ime, the s how petered out on its own, but not before it inspired Perkins to visit the Public Access studio.

"I realized after watching that show that Public Access was a p lace that allowed anyone to freely express themselves creatively," said Perkins.

He signed up for a training course at Public Access, they taught him the basics of TV production, and a short time later he launched his first Public Access show, *The Happy Dog Show*. He was still with KB Toys at the time and used toys to film raunchy s kits revolving around characters such as its host, Happy Dog, a dog puppet wearing sunglasses that told tasteless jokes; Mr. Waffles the alcoholic puppet; a homosexual police officer who liked to frisk people; a nd S atan the Weatherman who always gave the same weather report – "It is hot!" In a way, the show was before its time, a local precursor to the national hit, *South Park*.

He produced the show off and on for a decade. As he grew older, while the show stayed raunchy, it also matured. His jokes focused more on politics and less on pointless s ex acts and p otty h umor. He also became a larger p art of the show, c oming out from behind the puppets more and more, b antering with the puppets while poorly throwing his voice by obviously moving his mouth the entire time. Other times, he had friends and crew members control the puppets. He also revised his r ole a s t he c hainsaw chef and created new characters such as the Heathen Nun and White Chocolate the Pimp. He became the star of the show, not Happy Dog, and he renamed his program *The Happy Show*.

Then, in mid-2002, h e was g iven the n ews that would soon rock Tampa Bay. He said that Public Access officials told him that his show was too raunchy for the primetime 9 p.m. slot he held and would be moved t o 1 1 p .m. Public Access o fficials d enied t hat c laim. They s aid h is s how was moved because that was the timeslot it drew in the lottery, which is how they assigned timeslots to all their shows.

Perkins was furious. He had built a fan base at that timeslot. He thought the move would kill his momentum and he thought he was being censored.

"They said I was crude because I was cursing with puppets," he laughed. "Ridiculous. There was nothing crude about my show. But I thought, well, if they think I am crude, I will be crude." In his final episode in his primetime slot, he showed footage of one of his female friends naked and rubbing herself in the shower.

"It was my way of protesting," Perkins explained. It was his way of saying, "Damn the man!" At least one female viewer did not appreciate his form of free speech. The next day, she called her local representative, County Commissioner Ronda Storms, and complained. With that, The Great Public Access War of 2002 began.

Commissioner Storms was a conservative Republican who hitched her political wagon to God and the cause of cleaning up Hillsborough County's morals. Originally elected to the County Commission in 1998, she was up for reelection in 2002. Perkins provided her with the cause she had been looking for to propel her name into the newspaper and possibly ensure herself another four years on the County Commission.

After viewing the episode of his show featuring the girl in the shower, she filed a request with State Attorney Mark Ober to press obscenity charges against Perkins. She also wanted the county and city to pull its funding from Public Access for allowing such "obscenity" to be broadcast. Her requests made headlines in March 2002, putting both she and Perkins at the forefront of a censorship battle.

Perkins saw this as his opportunity to propel his show to new heights.

"I decided to push the issue a bit more and began showing nudity every week," he said. "If Public Access had never tried to censor me by moving my timeslot I would never have shown nudity. Then, if Ronda Storms had never made an issue out of it, I would never have shown it again. But the worst thing you can do to me is to challenge me. When you do, I fight back. Ronda Storms wanted to censor me so I kept shoving what she wanted to censor in her face – nudity."

He also made himself the face of Public Access, stating to the press that he was defending the station in the name of freedom of speech and because of all the good it provided to the community. He told the media that if the city and county pulled Public Access' funding, a lot of worthy organizations would suffer. He stood outside the County Center with a bullhorn and condemned Commissioner Storms for wanting to cut spending, and reminding anyone who would listen that the station was also used by organizations like the Boys & Girls Clubs to raise awareness of their causes.

However, despite claiming he had good intentions, he refused to stop airing nudity, even though that was the root of the problem. In fact, he stated that showing nudity helped the station rather than hindered it.

"By showing nudity, I think I did a lot of good for the station," Perkins stated. "Before my show, a lot of people did not know that the station existed. Suddenly, I'm all over the news and people are tuning in and see the other shows. Whenever the media would call me, I would 'pimp' the other shows, tell them about all the good programs that Public Access has. And then I would give them the names and email addresses of the producers of those shows. If you look back at the articles during that time, they often quote the producers of those shows and that had something to do with me."

Of course, Perkins will admit he wasn't only full of good intentions. He was having some devilish fun at the expense of Commissioner Storms. His show continually parodied her. He renamed his show, "The White Chocolate Show," to capitalize on his fame and he often ranted and raved about Commissioner Storms' desire to censor him and Public Access. He then added a new sidekick – Commissioner Storms herself. He taped a photo of her head onto a stick and had various members of his production crew act as the puppeteer.

"She was the best sidekick I had," Perkins laughed. "Whatever I said, she would be radically against. I'd say that I think freedom is great and she would chime in that freedom sucks and everyone should be locked in a cage. It was funny."

He produced skits that focused on Commissioner Storms' puppet. For instance, one of his other infamous puppets was Black Sock, a dirty black sock that represented a "clichéd black person." In one particular skit, Black Sock was taking a nap after a long day of picking cotton when the Commissioner Storms puppet showed up and unleashed a tirade of racial slurs toward him. In another skit, the Commissioner Storms puppet proposed to the rest of the County Commission—all of whom had their own puppets— that they should wear uniforms to each meeting. They voted in favor of the action and at the next meeting they were wearing KKK outfits. Following the meeting, the Commissioner Storms puppet invited the puppet depicting the African American County Commissioner Thomas Scott to meet her in private. The Commissioner Jan Platt puppet, which was cast as the intelligent member of the commission and was wearing Yoda ears to accentuate that point, thought something was amiss with the Commissioner Storms puppet's invitation and decided to investigate. She found the Commissioner Scott puppet hanging from a tree and the Commissioner Storms puppet pulling the rope.

"My favorites, though," said Perkins, holding his stomach as he laughed, "were when I had the Commissioner Storms puppet and a Satan puppet doing lines of coke together and when I had the Commissioner Storms puppet kill me in the shower in a takeoff of the *Psycho* scene."

"What made these skits so great," continued Perkins, "is that we had secret guests who would come on the show and do the Ronda Storms puppet's voice and you would be SHOCKED to know who some of the guests were. We never showed their faces but if we did, I think people would have been totally surprised."

After each episode of a show that poked fun at Commissioner Storms or showed nudity, Perkins would then send the tape to Commissioner Storms' office and write a fake note from a concerned citizen saying that she needs to get the show off the air.

"We were just egging her on," explained Perkins. "And she bought into it the entire time. But look, I was using her and she was using me. She saw me as her way to get attention to make a bigger name for herself, win reelection and then go on to bigger things. She was not innocent in all of this."

She would not leave Perkins alone. She kept attacking him and he kept winning the battles. At the height of their battle, Commissioner Storms and Perkins were guests on a local FOX 13 afternoon show that dealt with the "hot topic of the day." Perkins' attorney, Luke Lirot, who is best known for his legal defense of strip club king Joe Redner, pleaded with Perkins to leave the pimp outfit at home, reminding him that he was facing obscenity charges so it was best not to egg on the public on local TV. Perkins agreed, but could not pass up a chance to get under Commissioner Storms' skin on television. It was around Easter time that year and in keeping with the holiday spirit he made a "First Amendment Easter Basket" that contained such items as a copy of the Constitution, the First Amendment and more. He presented it to her at the beginning of the show and frazzled her.

"For the rest of the show she was off her game," said Perkins. "I got to her early. It was so easy to beat up on her."

In the meantime, public officials were turning on Commissioner Storms. Her fellow commissioners accused her of grandstanding when she asked to show an episode of Perkins' program during a County Commission meeting. In that particular episode, Perkins was reading from a children's book while flashing video images of naked women on the screen. Commissioner Storms said she wanted to show the episode to showcase to the commission the type of obscenity that was being broadcast on Public Access. The program was not broadcast in the meeting. The other commissioners thought she was just trying to keep her name in the headlines.

If that was her goal, it was working. Rarely did a day go by in which Perkins' or Commissioner Storms' names were not mentioned by a media outlet. Some national newspapers even picked up on the story.

Perhaps the most outlandish headline took place on May 3, 2002 when the *St. Petersburg Times* ran an article titled, "Storms: Show Using Sock Puppet to Threaten Her". In the previous week's episode of the *White Chocolate Show*, Black Sock told the Commissioner Storms puppet that he wanted to take her home and perform various sex acts on her. The real Commissioner Storms said she feared for her life after watching the episode.

"It was a sock puppet!" exclaimed Perkins with a sly grin on his face.

"She was so over the top."

The legal system agreed with Perkins. State Attorney Mark Ober declared that Perkins' show may have been offensive but was not criminally obscene and charges could not be pressed against Perkins or Public Access. He also stated that the episode that made Storms fear for her life could not be considered legally threatening to her.

Commissioner Storms would not give up. She was determined to defeat Perkins and Public Access. To do so, she began searching for other shows that could be deemed obscene.

In the meantime, Perkins continued to add time onto his 15 minutes of fame. On May 8, he announced he was running for County Commission District 3 against incumbent Commissioner Tom Scott. He announced in a typical White Chocolate manner. He arrived at the County Center around 11 a.m. with a group of friends who were carrying a box. Perkins said it was a gift for the Hillsborough County Commission. When he opened the box, Dave "The Dwarf" Flood, a popular 93.3 WFLZ personality, popped out holding Perkins' filing papers. At the time, Perkins swore he was serious about running. Today, he admits it was just a publicity stunt.

"I was just having fun bothering Ronda Storms," he said. He ended up dropping out of the race.

In June, after over a month of combing through tapes of various Public Access shows, Storms found the smoking gun she was looking for. On May 10, the show *Saheeb's Dream* showed video footage of the 1987 public suicide of Pennsylvania treasurer R. Budd Dwyer. Dwyer had been convicted of bribery, called a press conference to explain his actions and then committed suicide via firearm on live television. When *Saheeb's* host, Billy Willie, showed the footage, he could be heard saying, "Do it, do it" and then when blood flowed from Dwyer's head, Willie said, "Cool."

Any footage shown on Public Access required a release form from those appearing in it. Commissioner Storms said that because Dwyer was dead there was no way Willie could have acquired such a release. She demanded that Willie and Public Access be punished for that violation. She then said she would refer the tape to Ober to see if there were any other crimes committed during the airing of the show.

Commissioner Storms announced a press conference on June 14 to discuss the *Saheeb* episode and to again claim that the best way to stop such shows from airing in the future was to pull Public Access' funding. The press conference was not open to the public; press only.

Perkins' local fame had risen to the point that he was a regular guest on 93.3's afternoon show hosting a popular segment called "Pimp Slap a Bitch Thursdays." Listeners would call in and explain to Perkins why someone they knew needed to be "pimp-slapped." If Perkins agreed, he would simply exclaim, "Pimp slap that bitch!" and the sound of a screaming woman being slapped would follow. Through 93.3, Perkins received press credentials to Commissioner Storms' press conference. Dressed in full pimp uniform and accompanied by Dave "The Dwarf" Flood, Perkins burst into the press conference screaming that Commissioner Storms was trying to censor Tampa Bay. Commissioner Storms immediately retreated back to her office, calling a sudden end to her press conference.

A month later, on July 10, the *St. Petersburg Times* released a report stating that Commissioner Storms' crusade against Public Access had forced the State Attorney's Office to log 867 hours since March investigating the station, which equaled 11 weeks of full-time work for two employees at the office. *The Times* wrote that the State Attorney's Office estimated that it had spent $57,000 on the investigation. *The Times* also reported that technicians at the county's government access station had recorded 92 videotapes of public access shows since mid-March for Commissioner Storms and other county employees. *The Times* then wrote that the county normally charged $20 for videocassettes to recoup the cost of the tape and the time it took the technician to prepare it.

On July 20, Commissioner Storms could finally claim victory on one battlefront. Perkins was suspended by Public Access for a technical violation. He failed to run credits identifying him as a producer during a July 10 episode of his show. Perkins claimed that the reason behind the gaffe was that he fired a technician in the middle of the show and could not figure out how to run the credits properly. His excuse fell on deaf ears. Frustrated, rather than waiting out the suspension and then returning to the airwaves, Perkins opted to end his Public Access career and move on to other ventures.

These ventures revolved around the White Chocolate gimmick. He took to the internet to sell episodes of his show and even enjoyed a short stint as co-owner of a club in Ybor City with Joe Redner.

"Enjoyed a short stint is the key phrase," Perkins said. "We packed the place for the first few weeks when I was involved with it. Then we had a falling out over business issues and I was out. The club died without me."

He continued to hang onto the White Chocolate persona. He even came close to booking a spot on an episode of the then-popular *Jenny Jones Show*, but he turned the deal down due to differences over his role on the show. Show producers wanted him to be part of a lineup of pimps, real and fake, and a panel of experts had to figure out who the real pimps were. Perkins didn't want to be in the lineup, he wanted to be on the panel. When the show said no, he said no and moved on.

Despite getting Perkins off the airwaves, Commissioner Storms did not move on. In October she successfully convinced the County Commission to vote in favor of cutting $355,000 in aid it provided to Public Access. The commission said the cut was due to budgetary reasons. It was a short-lived victory. Shortly after the commission voted, *The St. Petersburg Times* quoted Commissioner Storms bragging, "They didn't get Al Capone for murder or racketeering. They got him for tax evasion."

A federal judge ruled that her comment was enough to reinstate Public Access' funding as it provided evidence that the vote was made to censor Public Access and not for budgetary reasons.

Perkins said it was around this time that he had a moment of clarity. He had numerous girlfriends at the time, but one in particular held his interest. She realized that the pimp act was just that – an act. She knew that Perkins was actually a decent and good man at heart who got a little too caught up in chasing those 15 minutes of fame. She told him that if he ever planned on getting married and having children with her or any other woman, he needed to leave White

Chocolate behind.

"I was sitting on my couch one night and had these strippers with me who had been crashing at my place," remembered Perkins. "I looked at them and realized that if I really wanted to I could become a pimp. I could have convinced them to let me pimp them out. I didn't want to be a real pimp. I wanted a family."

A few days later, he threw the White Chocolate costume away and got rid of all his girlfriends but one. She later became his wife and mother to his son. And like that, White Chocolate disappeared.

Commissioner Storms found ways to stay in the news using her newfound fame as the county's moral authority. She attacked the Hillsborough County Library System for having books on homosexuality. She called for ending county funding for Planned Parenthood.

Her popularity rose with ultra-conservative voters and in 2006 she was elected to the Florida Senate. In 2007, she again went after Public Access when she sponsored House Bill 529 that allowed cable companies to place access channels on their lowest, non-digital tier of service. Public Access in Tampa had historically been Bright House channels 19 and 20, channels viewers regularly surfed by. When this bill was passed, Tampa's Public Access was moved to Bright House channel 949, a channel few people surf past.

A funny thing happened to Perkins after he left White Chocolate behind. He found he had something in common with Ronda Storms. He also wanted to pursue a career in public service. And this time he was serious.

"If I learned one thing throughout the whole Public Access thing it is that our elected leaders don't do anything but find new ways to be elected," said Perkins. "They don't really care about the people. Then I looked around at my neighborhood and then saw New Tampa and realized that while my neighborhood is falling apart, New Tampa keeps getting money. I realized that if my neighborhood was ever going to get fixed, I had to take an active role."

He ran for a citywide council seat in 2003 and lost. He did not expect to win, however. A friend with political experience told him to put his name on the ballot and do nothing more. His friend said he had to admit that he had little chance of winning so not to spend money. But, by putting his name on the ballot, he could gauge what precincts he was best known in by which ones he won the most votes in.

"The election came and went and my friend said to take a map and color code it by how I did in each precinct – which ones did I come in first, second and so on," explained Perkins. "Then, he said to find a smaller district that encompasses those precincts."

And that is what he did. In 2007, he returned to the campaign trail, running for the City Council District 7 seat encompassing his neighborhoods, the area between Armenia and 50th Street, and New Tampa. He worked a tireless grassroots campaign, knocking on every door he could, stressing the ones "he could."

"They don't let you knock on doors in New Tampa," said Perkins. "It is a deed restricted area. But guess what? I won every precinct I did knock on doors in. I don't think I could have won New Tampa anyway. They would not have liked my message to give more of their money to the struggling neighborhoods."

He spent the next three years as a crime watch president of his neighborhood and then in 2011 decided to run yet again for district 7. He again walked the streets and knocked on doors, talking to as many people as he could personally. He even carried a giant notebook with him and jotted down everyone's concerns. He again lost, but made a positive stride – he made the runoff. New Tampa was again his Achilles Heel.

"After that election, I said I would never run again," he admitted. "I was tired. It was hard work and I thought that New Tampa would keep me from ever winning. But now I am thinking that was wrong of me to think. I really do want to help my neighborhood. The people running the city right now don't seem to care about it at all. This is 2011 and we have neighborhoods with dirt roads and no sidewalks. This is ridiculous. Don't tell me there is no money for it in the budget. Find it. These neighborhoods should be at the top of the city's to do list. So I'll run again. And next time I will bring some big guns to the fight. I'm going to hire a campaign consultant and other paid staff. I want to win. I want to help my neighborhood."

There will always be those who doubt that Charles Perkins is all grown up, but it truly does appear that he is. However, there will always be a little White Chocolate left him in. The devil hasn't been completely exorcised from his body. When asked if he would ever have a sit down with his former enemy, Ronda Storms, he said with a sly smile, "Of course. I'd love to see what she would order." It was obvious, though, that he had another answer in mind, one that he purposely held back.

He then ended the interview with, "The city of Tampa needs White Chocolate. It needs more real people in charge."

Perhaps he is right. Mayor White Chocolate The Public Access Pimp? That sounds just about right. It sounds just like a fitting mayor for Tampa – a true gentleman.

Chapter 13
The Ghost of Robert Anderson

"The moral of the Tampa story is this: if good citizens of a community shut their eyes to wholesale violation of a law – even if it is a law prohibiting something that a lot of people happen to like – law enforcement and honesty in public office will go to hell in a handcart. It happened in Tampa. It can happen anywhere." Estes Kefauver.

In the year 2011, he was being called a traitor. His sin – wanting the United States to live up to its name as the greatest Democracy in the world.

Al Fox is confused. He is confused as to why Americans are allowed to travel to China, a communist nation, but not Cuba on the grounds that it is a communist nation. He is confused as to why Americans were once allowed to travel to Taliban-controlled Afghanistan, one of the most oppressive nations in the history of mankind, but not Cuba on the grounds that it is oppressive.

Actually, Al Fox is not confused. He just likes to pose those questions to anyone who will listen in order to make his point that the United States' policy toward Cuba does not make sense.

"I am not going to sit here and tell you that the Cuban form of government is perfect. What I am telling you is that there are far more oppressive governments in this world and we are allowed to travel to them. In China, the government will break down a door in a home and if they find a woman eight months pregnant who did not get permission from the government to have a child, they will strap her down and abort the child. To me, that is a very serious human rights violation, yet we have diplomatic relations with them and not with Cuba."

Fox said that the Cuban citizens will tell you that their form of government is not perfect, but they support it, just like the United States is not perfect but we support it. They know if they turned on the Castros, the embargo would be lifted and their lives could perhaps be easier, but they refuse to do so. They will not be told by the United States how to run their country. The embargo has not worked, plain and simple; it has only fueled the Cuban people's fire to rebel against what the U.S. wants.

Fox knows this to be true because he has been to Cuba over 80 times and has had nine sit down meetings with Fidel Castro. But it is not necessary to visit Cuba that many times to see the truth. It is not necessary to meet Castro. It only takes one trip. It only takes a few days. It only takes a few conversations with regular Cuban citizen to learn the truth. And that is why Al Fox dedicates his life to taking Americans to Cuba; so they can see the truth for themselves.

Al Fox founded the Alliance for Responsible Cuba Policy Foundation in 1998 with its purpose being to help educate U.S. citizens on the truth about Cuba. The best way to do that, explained Fox, is to allow them to see Cuba for themselves. The Alliance helps U.S. citizens leap the numerous hurdles the U.S. government tosses in citizens' way when attempting to go to Cuba. While it is illegal to visit the Communist nation, there are ways for the everyday man and woman to go, such as via humanitarian, religious, people-to-people or journalistic visas. But the miles of paperwork can seem longer than the distance between Florida and Cuba, turning most off. Fox' Alliance is willing to do the legwork for you, without charge—except for the cost of the trip—and all Fox wants in exchange is for the returning traveler to talk publicly about their experience because "the government cannot deny the truth forever," he said. Since founding the alliance, he has taken mayors, congressman, senators and businessmen from around the nation.

All of them have returned and agreed with Fox' stance that the United States' policy with Cuba needed to be amended. For his efforts, he has been labeled a Communist and a traitor. There are some people in Tampa who would rather cross the street than walk by him.

"A traitor?" he laughed. "I am an American. We cannot tell the world that we are the freest, most democratic society on the planet and have a hypocritical policy toward Cuba. Many countries in the world believe we are phony. They say we do not really believe in democracy. I have heard this first hand."

"My motivation has nothing to do with helping Cubans like everybody thinks," he said, explaining that the money Tampa's airport could make off travel to Cuba and the money the port could make off trade would provide the city with a windfall of riches. His main reason for his fight, however, is because of his belief that the embargo and travel restriction is un-democratic and hurts the United States' image. "I don't want to help the people of Cuba. At the end of the day, the only motivation I truly care about are the people of the United States."

And he said if that makes him a traitor, then he would rather be a traitor.

Books were banned in Hillsborough County in the year 2011.

It began in 2005 when ignorant citizens were outraged over gay and lesbian books being on display at Hillsborough County libraries. They took their cause to the Hillsborough County Commission and, led by Commissioner Ronda Storms, they voted to ban the county government from acknowledging gay pride. Books promoting such a lifestyle can no longer be on display at county libraries.

Gay and lesbian coalitions have fought the ban and have yet to see a victory, mostly due to the fact that they have not been able to rally the masses behind their cause.

In 2012, censorship continues to be alive and well in Hillsborough County and no one seems to care.

Kevin White had the world at his feet. He was handsome, articulate, outgoing, charismatic, educated and was born into the most beloved and prominent African American families in the history of the city of Tampa – the White family.

Its patriarch, Moses White, helped integrate the city and took care of any down on his luck member of the African American community in whatever way he could, via helping find employment or providing them with a job.

Most never forgot the good that Moses White did for the community and they paid him back by supporting his family in any way they could. With his personality and credentials, Kevin White could have run the city. However, he never could stay on the straight and narrow.

In November 2011, he was found guilty on seven of 10 corruption charges. While serving as a Hillsborough County Commissioner, White accepted bribes to help wrecker companies get on a law enforcement towing rotation. At the time he took the bribes, he chaired the Public Transportation Commission, a board that regulates wreckers and other vehicles for hire.

What made this incident so shocking was that people were actually shocked when news broke of White taking bribes. Kevin White was not new to controversy, yet despite multiple blemishes on his name he continued to rise up the ranks of Tampa politics.

He had a stint in the Navy that lasted just 56 days. As a Tampa Police officer he often found trouble. He was flagged for violating the city chase policy when a citizen was hurt in a wreck his chase caused. He was later accused of, while in uniform, visiting the home of a man with whom he'd been in an auto accident and demanding money from him.

Despite this shady past, he was elected to the Tampa City Council in 2003. The two most notable moments of his term on City Council were when he unsuccessfully tried to secure a 23 percent raise for city council members at a meeting that did not have any citizens or members of the media in attendance and when a real estate swindler admitted he donated thousands of dollars in illegal contributions to White's 2003 campaign.

Somehow, no matter how much controversy was piled upon White's name, he continued to find political success. In 2006 he won a seat on the Hillsborough County Commission and his term lived up to his dark past. He was convicted of using campaign money to purchase expensive suits and was convicted of sexually harassing his legislative aide. It was also during this term that he accepted the bribes. In 2010, before the accusations of bribery came out, he lost a bid for reelection. The sexual harassment charges were believed to have been the factor for his loss. However, one has to wonder how it took so long for the Tampa Bay community to wise up to a swindling politician's corrupt ways.

Tampa's 2011 mayoral election was supposed to be the standard for how politicians should treat one another. The race for mayor of Tampa had one of the most crowded yet respected fields in the history of the city. Political pundits agreed that whoever won the election, the city would be in good hands. All five candidates were immensely qualified to lead the city of Tampa for the next four to eight years.

Dick Greco was a former four-time mayor, 1967-1974 and 1995-2003, whose many accomplishments included integrating City Hall, bringing an end to the illegal bolita rings, rebuilding Ybor City, saving the Convention Center from financial ruin and turning downtown Tampa from a sleepy corner of the city into a thriving community.

Bob Buckhorn was a top aide to former Mayor Sandy Freedman, a former City Councilman and head of his own lobbying firm. During his terms as a councilman, he was credited with cracking down on Tampa's prostitution and rave problems.

Rose Ferlita was a former city councilman and then-county commissioner who also ran a successful pharmacy. Throughout her political career, she had a reputation for being a defender of neighborhoods, animals and bullied children. She supported gay pride events, a homeless tent city and saving the county's division for wetlands protection.

Tom Scott was an ordained minister, head of the 34th Street Church of God that boasted 900 members, former county commissioner and then-city councilman. He served three years as the County Commission chairman, selected by his fellow board members, including Republicans. He also was selected by his fellow council members three times as City Council chairman.

Ed Turanchick was an attorney, a former county commissioner and a leader in the fight to bring light rail to Tampa. He was best known for, while a county commissioner, leading the successful effort to end 70 years of regional water wars, which culminated in the formation of a new regional authority and over a billion dollars of new water supply projects.

Politics had become an ugly profession throughout the United States in the years directly prior to that mayoral election. Elections were dirty, more about mudslinging and name calling than platforms. And once politicians were in office, it seemed they had to spend as much time defending every decision they made as they did making decisions. Party leaders found fault in everything an elected official from the opposing party did. An elected official could have cured cancer and been slammed by the opposing party for costing the medical industry the money it made off chemotherapy. Politics no longer seemed as though it was about helping people. It was only about helping your party – Republican or Democrat.

But Tampa's 2011 mayoral race was supposed to be different. Because each candidate was so well qualified and so respected, there was no reason for mudslinging to be brought into the election. They could all debate the issues and what needed to be done to better the city of Tampa. They were all too respected to resort to personal attacks.

They agreed to set the example for the rest of the nation for how political candidates should conduct themselves. They agreed that the election would be gentlemanly. And in a way, it was; it was as gentlemanly as the gun duels that solved debates in the Wild West.

Dick Greco, the man who integrated City Hall, was painted as a racist by the media and two of his fellow candidates. At one debate, he innocently compared a near racial riot that occurred when he was mayor in 1968 to "panty raids." He meant that the would-be rioters were only acting out because they were following the lead of other cities with violent racial strife, just as college kids during his day would panty raid a co-ed dorm because they heard of others doing it. His choice of words was poor, but to label him a racist for such was ridiculous. No one was hurt in the 1968 riot, but the next day the media referenced a riot that occurred in 1967 that did turn deadly. That particular riot did not even occur when Greco was mayor.

Then, a few days later at another debate, the candidates were asked a light hearted question, "Which candidate would each appoint as the designated driver if you went out drinking together at MacDinton's?" MacDinton's is a popular college-age bar.

Greco, Bob Buckhorn and Ed Turanchik all answered the obvious – Tom Scott, an ordained minister who also does not drink.

The next question was, "What would you hire the candidate to your left to do if elected mayor?" Tom Scott was to Greco's left and when it was his turn to answer, he jokingly said, "My driver to take me home from MacDinton's." The crowd erupted in laughter, as did all the other candidates, including Tom Scott. The forum went on and everyone went home thinking nothing newsworthy came out of the event.

When the city woke up the next morning, Tom Scott had changed his tune. Suddenly, he did not understand Greco's joke. He labeled it as a racist remark. Scott is an African American and pretended that he thought Greco's joke that he should be his driver meant he should be his slave. Scott laughed at it the night before. There was even video proof of him and the audience laughing at the joke.

"I was shocked," Tom was quoted as saying. "I'm the chairman of the city council and I have served several times as chair of the county commission, and the best answer he could come up with is a driver ... I think it shows he is beyond his time. He didn't seem to understand that his comments might be viewed as offensive."

Scott knew it was a joke yet he was parlaying into something more. Another candidate weighed in on it as well – Ed Turanchik.

"It's just not appropriate. It's just out of touch," he said to the papers. "You don't do or say those things."

Rumor has it that shortly after the forum, Ed Turanchik called Tom Scott at home and began pushing his buttons. Rumor has it that Turanchik told Scott that he should be offended by the comment because it belittled him as an African American that one of the candidates, Greco, would think he was only qualified to be a driver. Turanchik knew it was a joke, as did Scott. But a light went off in Turanchik's head that night – he could use Greco's comment to try to knock him down another peg or two. Scott realized what Turanchik was up too and agreed with his plan.

Greco was the man who integrated City Hall in the 1960s and 70s. Greco hired the first African American firefighters; the first African American assistant city attorney, Warren Dawson; the first African American secretary in the mayor's office, Evelyn Wilson; and the first African American head of the Tampa Housing Authority, Howard Harris. In 1969, as many as 60 new African Americans were hired by the city government for administrative jobs. Two of his best friends – Bob Gilder and Moses White – were Civil Rights pioneers in Tampa. Yet, Greco was being painted as a racist.

Then, just days before the General Election, an anonymous flier falsely accusing Greco of bankrupting the city while he was mayor from 1995-2003 was mailed to t housands o f v oters. T he f lier w as f unded by a P olitical Action Committee (PAC). This has become a popular way for candidates to attack their opponents without getting blood on their own hands. Their supporters create a PAC and use the money to smear the names of their candidate's opponents. Then the guilty candidate can claim he or she had no idea who funded the PAC. If their supporters are outed, the candidate can claim they did not condone such an action and never asked for them to do it.

It was never discovered who funded the anti-Greco flyer.

Following the primary election that saw Ferlita and Buckhorn as the winners who had to face off in a runoff election, an anti-Ferlita flyer was released and tied to a Buckhorn campaign worker. The flyer casted doubt on Ferlita's commitment to family values because she's single; it described her as "Unmarried. Unsure. Unelectable." It had nothing to do with the issues of being mayor. Despite it being tied to a supporter, Buckhorn denied knowledge of it.

Ferlita r esponded w ith a n egative c ampaign o f h er o wn. S he a ired television co mmercials c riticizing B uckhorn a s an " elitist" a nd "failed businessman." Ferlita's campaign turned so ugly that then-Mayor Pam Iorio, who had remained quiet up to that point in the election, stepped onto the playing field and endorsed Buckhorn, stating Ferlita's ugly campaigning as her reason.

Buckhorn won the election and the entire city lost, but not because

Buckhorn was not qualified. Buckhorn has been a tremendous mayor. The city lost because d espite t he p re-election claims o f k eeping t he e lection c ivil a nd gentlemanly, it was anything but that.

What was saddest about the entire ordeal was that no one seemed to care. There was not a public outcry about the anonymous flyers. There was no shock over the man who integrated City Hall being labeled a racist. People just accepted that such election tactics were the norm and went about their lives. The belief that politics is supposed to be dirty was perhaps a contributing factor behind only 22 percent o f Tampa's 190,000 registered v oters t urning out for the runoff election. Perhaps people are tired of it. But if they are, why don't they do anything to stop it?

Has anything really changed in Tampa?

Some would say that it is unfair to compare today's community with the dirty elections, shady politicians and corruption of yesteryear. Not only is it fair to compare the two generations, it is spot on to write that nothing has really changed. The names and places are different, but the crimes remain the same.

Elections were c orrupt in t he early 1900s when Charlie W all ran the city. Many citizens would say that elections are corrupt today. The form of corruption practiced today is legal, but it is corrupt nonetheless.

Kevin White had the world at his feet, as did Gene Holloway. They both chose the easy path and learned the hard way that there is no easy path to success. Carlos Carbonell was called a t raitor for s upporting what h e thought would be a Democratic Cuba. Al Fox is called a t raitor for w anting t he United S tates t o act more like a Democracy. Ronda Storms tried to c ensor Public A ccess t elevision. She did censor the Hillsborough County libraries.

Nothing has changed at all in Tampa.

"The moral of the Tampa story is this: if good citizens of a community shut their eyes to wholesale violation of a law – even if it is a law prohibiting something that a lot of people happen to like – law enforcement and honesty in

public office will go to hell in a handcart. It happened in Tampa. It can happen anywhere." Estes Kefauver.

That is perhaps the most telling quote ever written or said about Tampa. The reason nothing has changed, the reason Tampa is faced with the same issues today as it did at the turn of the century, is because people choose to ignore their problems. They want to pretend Tampa is all sunshine when it in fact has quite a bit of darkness. While Tampa has different eras of darkness, each has the same common theme – indifference. As it was in the 1500s, the area known as Tampa is still one full of gentleman. While there are still many stories from the past that can be written, their will surely be many more occurring in the future.

Perhaps nothing will ever change...Need more proof?

In 2010 and 2011, close to two dozen homes were set on fire. Headlines called the man behind them the "Ybor City Firebug".

About the Author

Born a nd r aised i n T renton, N ew J ersey, P AUL G UZZO m oved to Tampa, Fl. in 1999. He s pent 10 y ears as h ead writer at La Gaceta Newspaper - the nation's ONLY t ri-linguel n ewspaper - where he wrote a weekly profile on Tampa Bay's most p rolific p ersonalities, from mayors and g overnors t o CIA a gents and military generals to artists and athletes. He continues to work for La Gaceta on a freelance b asis. He i s a lso s enior w riter for C igar City M agazine, a Tampa-based history magazine. Along with his brother, he has produced numerous independent films t hat h ave s hown a ll o ver the world, a nd have won dozens of awards along the way.

www.ingramcontent.com/pod-product-compliance
Lightning Source LLC
Chambersburg PA
CBHW070753290326
41931CB00011BA/1994